# *The Manufacture of Sausages*
*The First and Only Book on Sausage Making Printed In English*

*by Jas. C. Duff*

**with an introduction by Sam Chambers**

*This work contains material that was originally published in 1899.*

*This publication is within the Public Domain.*

*This edition is reprinted for educational purposes
and in accordance with all applicable Federal Laws.*

*Introduction Copyright 2017 by Sam Chambers*

# Self Reliance Books

Get more historic titles on animal and stock breeding, gardening and old fashioned skills by visiting us at:

# http://selfreliancebooks.blogspot.com/

## *Introduction*

I am pleased to present another book on the curing and preservation of meat on the farm or in the kitchen.

The work is in the Public Domain and is re-printed here in accordance with Federal Laws.

As with all reprinted books of this age that are intended to perfectly reproduce the original edition, considerable pains and effort had to be undertaken to correct fading and sometimes outright damage to existing proofs of this title. At times, this task is quite monumental, requiring an almost total "rebuilding" of some pages from digital proofs of multiple copies. Despite this, imperfections still sometimes exist in the final proof and may detract from the visual appearance of the text.

I hope you enjoy reading this book as much as I enjoyed re-publishing and making it available to fanciers again.


With Regards,

Sam Chambers

# THE BUTCHER'S GUIDE

### PORK.
1. Leg
2. Hind-loin
3. Fore-loin
4. Spare-rib
5. Shoulder
6. Brisket

### LAMB.
1. Leg
2. Shoulder
3. Loin
4. Loin, chump-end
5. Rack
6. Breast
7. Neck

### BEEF.
1. Neck
2. Clod
3. Chuck ribs
4. Middle ribs
5. Fore-rib
6. Shoulder
7. Brisket
8. Thin flank
9. Veiny piece
10. Loin
11. Rump
12. Aitch-bone
13. Round
14. Mouse-round
15. Thick flank
16. Shank

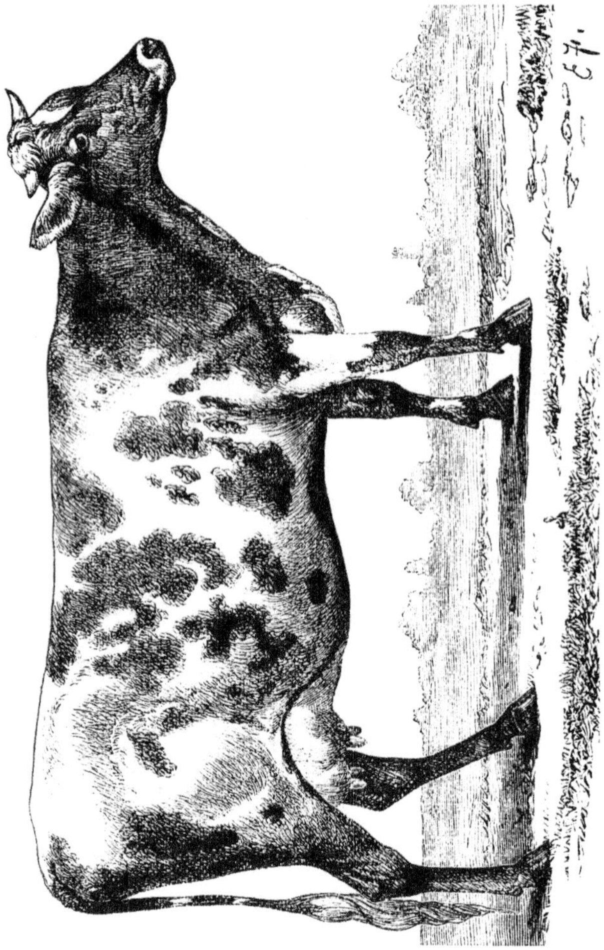

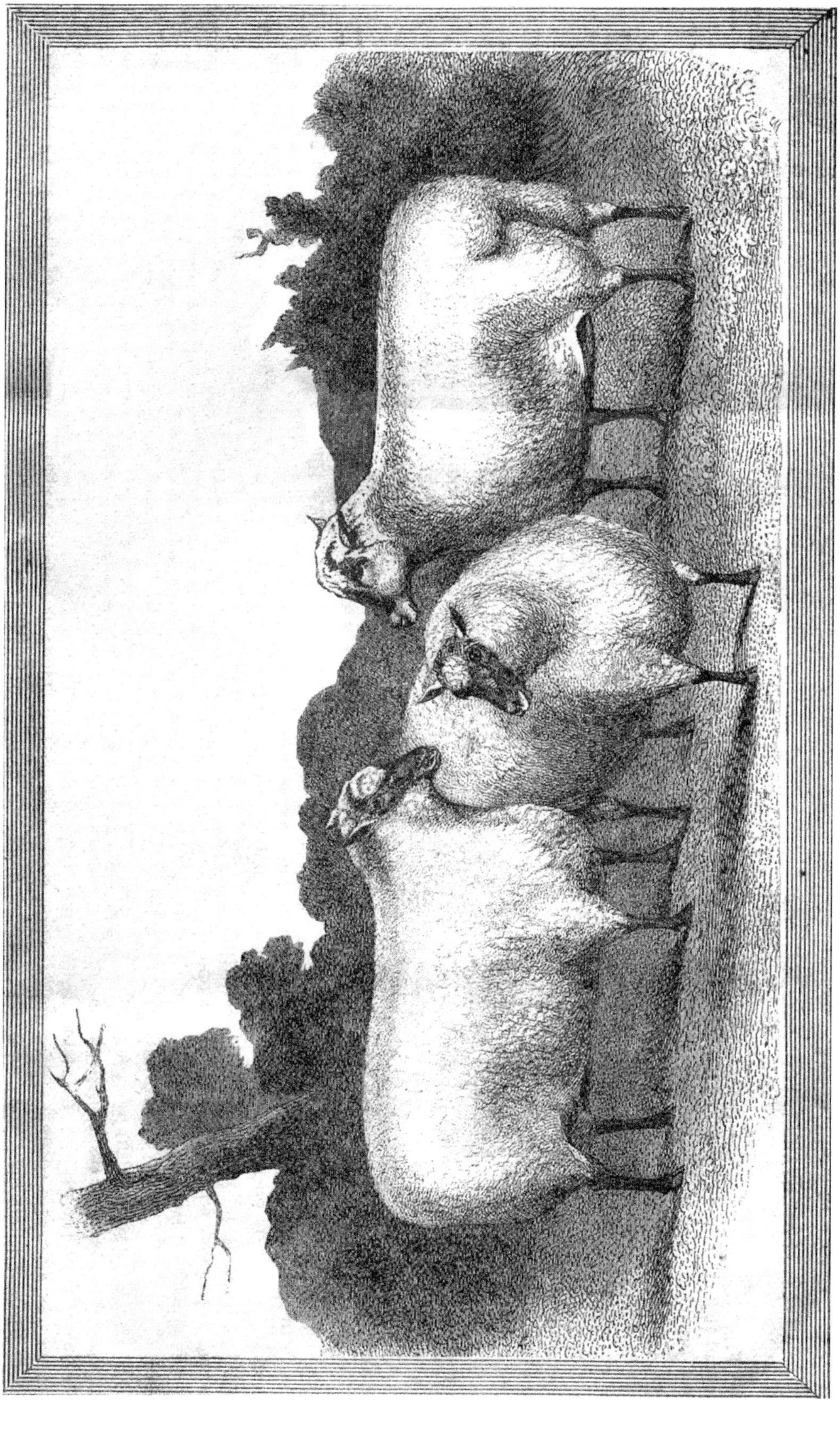

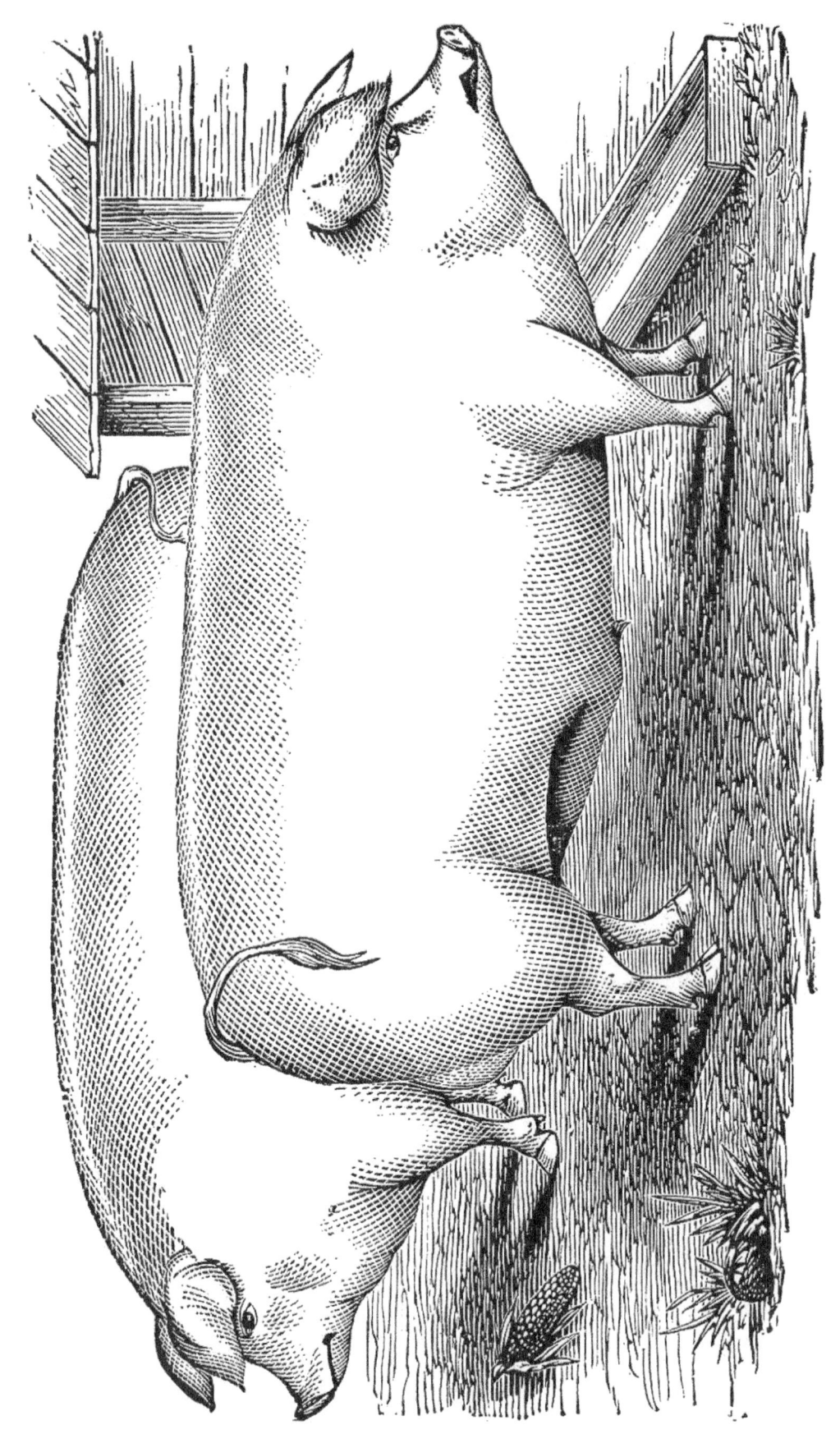

CHESTER WHITE HOGS—OLD STYLE.

# PREFACE

THE object for which this book is written is a practical one and to present in a simple and a convenient form the recipes and methods which are in daily use by the most successful sausagemakers and packers.

It has been the aim to present the subject in such form as will enable the beginner to acquire a more or less thorough insight into the matter, and permit him to engage in the successful and profitable manufacture of sausages. Many methods in vogue are needlessly complicated and laborious, involving unnecessary expense. These have herein been curtailed and simplified as much as possible, and still give reliable results.

Some of the recipes in the book have, from time to time, been published in THE NATIONAL PROVISIONER. To these have been added many new and valuable ones, which have been found reliable and of sterling worth. While each formula may be consulted for individual information, the whole may be regarded as indispensable to the beginner who wishes to engage in this industry.

No attempt has been made by the writer to give an exhaustive treatise on the subject, but it is believed that the book will prove valuable, not only to the experienced manufacturer, but also to those desirous of becoming practical sausagemakers.

# THE MANUFACTURE OF SAUSAGES.

## TABLE OF CONTENTS.

| CHAPTER | PAGE |
|---|---|
| I—Sausagemaking | 11 |
| II—Spices and Seasonings | 15 |
| III—Meats | 19 |
| IV—Blood Colors | 25 |
| V—Casings | 29 |
| VI—Stuffing | 34 |
| VII—Cooking | 37 |
| VIII—Smoking | 40 |
| IX—Fillers | 41 |
| X—Preservatives | 51 |
| XI—General Information | 59 |
| XII—Sausage Recipes | 65, 129 |

### RECIPES.

| | |
|---|---|
| Appetite Sausage | 84 |
| Bayonne Bladder Ham | 120 |
| Bayonne Ham | 120 |
| Beef Sausage | 70 |
| Block Sausage, Best | 96 |
| Blood Sausage, Common | 114 |
| Blood Sausage, Berliner | 113 |
| Bloodwurst | 115 |
| Bock Sausage | 108 |
| Bock Sausage, Another Recipe | 109 |
| Bologna Sausage | 126 |
| Bologna Sausage, Another Recipe | 126 |
| Bologna Sausage, German | 127 |
| Boudin Blanc (White Sausage) | 77 |
| Brain Sausage | 110 |
| Brain Sausage, Another Recipe | 110 |
| Brunswick Sardine Liver Sausage | 97 |
| Brussels Mosaic Sausage | 88 |
| Bulk Sausage | 129 |
| Calf Sweetbread Galantine | 124 |
| Cambridge Sausage | 129 |
| Coblenzer Knack Sausage | 80 |
| Conedini | 78 |
| Decorated Ham | 119 |
| Frankfort Fried Sausage | 75 |
| Frankfort Liver Sausage, Common | 99 |
| Frankfort Liver Sausage, Fine | 98 |
| Frankfort Liver Sausage, Hausmacher | 98 |
| Frankfort Pork Sausage | 71 |
| Frankfort Sausage | 105 |
| Frankfort Sausage—Another Recipe | 71 |
| Frankfort Tongue Press Cheese | 87 |
| Frankfort Yellow Sausage | 106 |
| Frankforter Blood Stomach | 105 |
| Frankforts | 74 |
| French Fricadelles | 110 |
| Fricadellen | 109 |

## TABLE OF CONTENTS.

| | PAGE |
|---|---|
| Garlic Sausage | 106 |
| Garlic Sausage, Best | 107 |
| Goose Liver Galantine | 123 |
| Goose Liver Pie, Finest Strassberger | 103 |
| Goose Liver Sausage | 102 |
| Goose Liver Sausage—See Strassberg Truffle, etc. | — |
| Ham, Chicken and Tongue Sausage | 83 |
| Hamburger Dried Smoked Beef | 80 |
| Hamburger Knack Sausage | 80 |
| Head Cheese, Common | 86 |
| Head Cheese, Another Recipe | 87 |
| Head Cheese, Finest | 87 |
| Hog's Head, Stuffed Parisian | 116 |
| Horseradish Sausage | 108 |
| Jauer Sausage | 115 |
| Jauer Sausage—Another Recipe | 115 |
| Kidney Sausage | 111 |
| Kidney Sausage, Smoked | 111 |
| Knack Sausage, Silesian or Breslau | 108 |
| Lachs Schlinken | 125 |
| Liver Cheese | 85 |
| Liver Sausage | 97 |
| Liver Sausage, Brunswick | 101 |
| Liver Sausage, Gothaer | 100 |
| Liver Sausage with Onions | 99 |
| Liver Sausage, Schweriner | 104 |
| Liver Sausage, Schweriner—Another Recipe | 104 |
| Lyonnaise Sausage | 74 |
| Mainzer Red Sausage | 78 |
| Mett Sausage | 93 |
| Mett Sausage, Best | 94 |
| Mett Sausage, Brunswick | 94 |
| Mett Sausage, Brunswick—Another Recipe | 94 |
| Mortadelli, Finest—Dutch Style | 121 |
| Mortadelli, Italian | 122 |
| Munich Cervelat | 93 |
| Oldenburger Rulken | 113 |
| Oxford Sausage | 70 |
| Parisian Jelly | 117 |
| Parisian Ham Sausage | 118 |
| Polish Sausage | 127 |
| Pork Sausage | 69 |
| Pork Sausage—Another Recipe | 69, 70 |
| Pressed Sausage | 89 |
| Roestwurst | 76 |
| Rollepöhse (George Sausage) | 112 |
| Salami di Verona | 92 |
| Salami—Genuine Italian Recipe | 91 |
| Salami—Hungarian | 91 |
| Sardelle Sausage | 85 |
| Saucisses de Boulogne | 81 |
| Saucisse, Parisian | 82 |
| Smoked Pork Sausage | 70 |
| Strassberg Truffle and Goose Liver Sausage | 101 |
| Strassburger Sausage | 77 |
| Summer Sausage | 95, 128 |
| Swiss Landjaeger | 123 |
| Thuringian Red Sausage | 79 |
| Tongue Sausage | 83 |
| Tongue, Gothaer | 83 |
| Veal Sausage | 90 |
| Vienna Kreen Sausage | 76 |
| Vienna Sausage (Wienerwurst) | 72 |
| Vienna Sausage (Wienerwurst)—Another Recipe | 73 |
| White Pudding, North of England | 121 |
| Seasonings for Sausages | 130, 131 |

## INTRODUCTION

Not many years ago the sausage was regarded with much suspicion and distrust, and as a final resort for material which from any cause became unsalable or of questionable value or condition. This impression, which held until comparatively recent years happily for both producer and consumer, no longer exists. That the prejudice has disappeared is greatly to the advantage of the latter, as it enables him to purchase, at a moderate cost, a good healthful article of food, having all the nutritive value of the whole cuts of meat.

Good sausage can be made only from good material, and manufacturers, with a lively appreciation of this fact, use the greatest care in the selection of their stock. To the high class of goods, we may say universally used, corroborative evidence is given by the fact of the enormous demand and increasing consumption of sausages and kindred products in this country. No mystery obtains in their manufacture, and sausagemakers, as a rule, cordially welcome inspection of their establishments and of the ingredients used.

Like most of the packinghouse products of to-day, the meats used in the production of sausages are from animals rigidly inspected before and after slaughter, and are as free from all objection as are the choicest of prime cuts.

Only the best pork and beef are now used, and for this reason the confidence of the public has been deservedly earned.

When every care is taken to hold this assurance, as this industry is making such rapid strides, affording such a profitable outlet for hearts, cheek meat, trimmings, etc., it is obvious that it would be worse than imbecility to abuse this well-merited and substantial trust.

This branch is to-day one of the leading features of the pork and beef packing industry. There have been periods when the sausage department has been depended upon to make the yearly profits of the whole establishment. In general, it is the one place of the whole packing-house from which a good profit is expected and obtained.

There is no reason why the small meat dealer should not utilize his trimmings and surplus fats to this good advantage instead of tanking or selling them to the renderer. With a small outlay the necessary appliances can be purchased for a complete plant, which will net a handsome return upon the investment. A very important point not to be overlooked in this connection is the fact that there is practically no waste in the production of sausages.

The art of sausagemaking has reached, in this country, a high degree of perfection, which is due as much to the efforts of the small progressive meat dealer and butcher as to those of the largest packer. Both present to the consumer an attractive, savory and palatable article of food.

15 Katharinen Strasse  Boulcott Street  47-53 St. John Street
Hamburg, Germany  Wellington, N. Z.  London, Eng.

ESTABLISHED OVER 30 YEARS

# S. OPPENHEIMER & CO.

449 Wabash Avenue  96 and 98 Pearl Street
Chicago, Ill.  New York

MANUFACTURERS, EXPORTERS AND IMPORTERS
OF ALL KINDS OF

## SAUSAGE CASINGS

Pure Spices, Prepared Spices, Sausage Seasoning, Herbs, Potato Flour, Berlin Flour, Bread Meal, Saltpetre, Preserving Powder, French Carbon, Smokine, Fixtures, Tools, Machinery and Lard Pails.

———— Best in the World! ————

The BUFFALO CHOPPERS, SILENT CUTTERS, SPICE MILLS LARD MIXERS and KETTLES, STUFFERS, Etc.

JOHN E. SMITH'S SONS,
Buffalo, N. Y., U. S. A.

We make a Full Line of FANS, both Electric & Belt

Also, MOTORS for running Choppers and Fans.

Send For Catalogues and Prices to

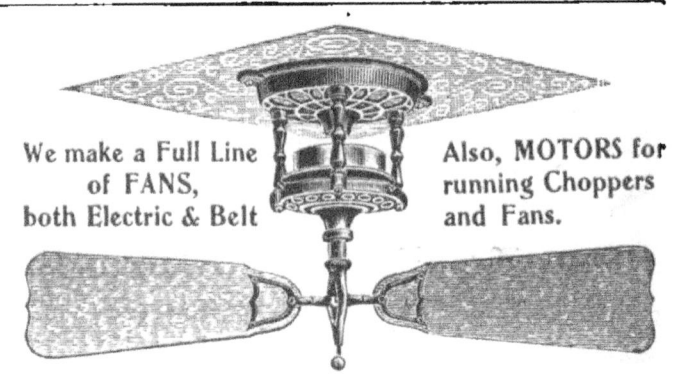

HUNTER FAN & MOTOR CO., FULTON, N. Y.

# I

# SAUSAGEMAKING

## SAUSAGEMAKING

To obtain a good sausage there must be cleanliness in all operations, good meat, good seasonings and spices.

A requisite in sausage manufacture essential to success, is absolute cleanliness everywhere and at all times. This cannot be too strongly emphasized. When the operations for the day are completed, tables, benches, floors, and all machinery and utensils used, should be thoroughly washed and scrubbed with scalding hot water to which has been added some sal soda. This removes the grease and other accumulations of the day from these articles, and prevents them becoming foul, and breeding places for flies and germs. It also leaves everything in condition to start work again without any unnecessary delay.

After washing the cutters, stuffers, etc., rub over all the iron and steel parts which come in contact with the meat, with a cloth saturated with cottonseed oil or pure neatsfoot oil to prevent formation of rust. The former oil is in general use because of its lesser cost.

After floors and benches are scraped and scrubbed, before they become perfectly dry, salt should be scattered very freely over them. By this they are kept sweet and in a presentable condition.

The value of water as a cleanser and disinfectant is too well known to need discussion. Its plentiful use at all times is a safeguard against foul and disagreeable odors. An important item to be considered in connection with every establishment of this kind, is a reliable supply of good water free from (and guarded against) future contamination. Ample provision for good sewers and drainage must also be made. Wherever practicable, tile instead of wood should be used for this purpose, as the latter will in a short time become very foul, and, instead of eliminating conditions that tend to create nuisances, become nuisances themselves.

All waste and wash water should be conducted to catch-basins where any grease carried by the water and washings will be caught and saved. The catch-basin is an important adjunct to all places handling animal products, and it saves, annually, many thousand pounds of grease, which otherwise by escaping into the sewer, would become a total loss.

In this, as in nearly all manufactures, the cost of production decreases correspondingly, with the increased quantity produced. As the work proceeds, methods and skill improve, and the quality of the article becomes better and more uniform. If the factory is well equipped and properly conducted, the result is certain to produce a class of high grade sausages and kindred products.

Our Many Years' Experience in the Manufacture of

# Spices, Herbs, Seasonings, Etc.

Especially for

## SAUSAGEMAKERS AND PROVISIONERS

Enables us to Supply the Trade with the Very Finest Grade of these Specialties.

Our Machinery is the Most Modern.

Our Labor the Most Skilled.

## B. FISCHER & CO.,

"FISCHER MILLS,"

393, 395 and 397 Greenwich Street,    NEW YORK.

INSPECTION OF OUR PLANT SOLICITED.

---

# F. R. FARRINGTON & CO., EQUITABLE MILLS

**SPICES**

ALL KINDS OF WHITE PEPPER A SPECIALTY.

Everything in the way of Spices, that is used by Packers, Provisioners, Sausagemakers, Butchers and Mince Meat Manufacturers.

When in want, drop us a line and we will gladly send samples and quotations.

## 244-246 Greenwich St.,

Telephone, 4723 Cortlandt.    **NEW YORK.**

# II

# SPICES AND SEASONINGS

## SPICES AND SEASONINGS

The principal flavoring substances of spices are the essential oils they contain. These, when exposed to the air, rapidly volatilize and render worthless the remaining part of the spice. To prevent this deterioration, spices should be kept in tightly covered cans or boxes where they retain their strength and are also protected from dust and other impurities in the air.

The employment of cheap spices and seasonings should be avoided if for no other reason than their ultimate costliness. This class of goods eventually proves much more expensive than high grade, pure spices. It takes a greater quantity of weaker spices to attain the desired result. In addition to this, goods made with them give little or no satisfaction and are never a superior product.

In this age of sophistication the purchase of a small spice mill for grinding the whole spices is a commendable investment. With this, no more need be ground than is required for each day's output. Prepared in this way, spices are very efficient and fragrantly pungent and as such, will produce a more finely flavored sausage.

Many purchase spices in the open market, already ground. When a consumer has not the means at hand for testing them and ascertaining their actual value, they should be obtained from reliable dealers of known reputation. If, however, there is reason to doubt their purity, before using, it is best to have them examined by a competent chemist. The sausage manufacturer can, with profit to himself, select good spices for his purposes. The finished product containing these costs but little more, gives better satisfaction to the trade and the increased sales will fully compensate the maker for the slight additional expense of first-class ingredients.

A most important point to be observed in the manufacture of sausages is the method of incorporating spices and seasonings in the mixtures. An even and uniform distribution of these throughout the mass must be obtained and this is accomplished by *thorough* kneading.

A very necessary thing in all well conducted factories is a small scale, sensitive to a quarter of an ounce. This is used for weighing accurately the various proportions of the spices and seasonings. Here, no "rule of thumb" or guess work should be permitted, as the exact quantities of these ingredients make the requisite delicate aroma. Variations from the indicated weights should be guarded against, for any undue amount of one might entirely change the desired flavor. By careful weighing, a uniformly seasoned product is always obtained, an important factor not to be overlooked.

The spices and seasonings mostly employed in sausage-making are:

Black Pepper.
White Pepper.
Shot Pepper.
Cayenne Pepper.
Coriander Seed.
Marjoram.
Sage.
Basil.
Thyme.

---

Salt.
**Powdered Saltpetre.**
Ground Mace.
" Nutmeg.
" Allspice.

Ground Ginger.
   "     Cinnamon.
   "     Cloves.

Onions.
Garlic.
Shallots.

Many others are used in special cases, as for instance, cardamom, truffles, etc., but their use is very limited.

When herbs used for seasoning are too moist to rub up well, they should be placed in a cloth bag and hung up in a warm, dry place, until the excess of moisture has evaporated. When in proper condition, herbs are easily and quickly powdered to the degree of fineness needed in mixing. With these, as with spices, care should be taken to keep them dry and to protect them from a dusty or a moist atmosphere.

Further valuable information will be found on pages 130, 131 regarding seasoning mixtures.

# III

# MEATS

| 1861 | **The Only Original.** | 1899 |

Bell's Spiced Sausage Seasoning and Bell's Sausage Dressing are the product of over thirty-five years' experience. They are made under the personal supervision of Mr. Bell, who made sausages as far back as 1857. They are the direct result of practical experience. They are practical, and never fail to season that way. All other spiced Seasonings that have come and gone and that are now, are but puny imitations of the genuine original.

## BELL'S SPICED SAUSAGE SEASONINGS

Nothing but the best spiced Seasoning can make the best Sausages.

**SPECIAL NOTICE:** Unscrupulous concerns have been taking orders ostensibly for Bell's, and billing them as such, while actually filling the orders with the cheap, disastrous, unsatisfactory imitations. As such roguery is but a cloaked form of robbery, and as it must work havoc to the sausage trade, we have withdrawn Bell's from all supply houses except four honorable houses. We will name these on request. Your orders for Bell's will be filled by these or any wholesale grocer or direct by us. But be sure you specify and get Bell's. Refuse all others. Substitution is the fraud of the age. It should be abolished. Every time you order Bell's you help stamp out substitution.

**REMEMBER** Bell's is a combination Spiced Seasoning; gives better effect than a dozen varieties, easier, cheaper. We grind our own spices and nothing but the best is used. Our catalogue tells you how to make the best sausages. It's free for the asking. State what kind of seasoning you need and a small sample will be mailed free. Don't fail to secure our prices.

**BELL'S PATENT PARCHMENT LINED SAUSAGE BAGS** The most popular because the most practical. Some packers order in lots of 50,000. That tells the story plainly. Prices and samples on application.

**BELL'S MEAT CUTTERS.** No. 1 will cut 100 lbs. pork in one minute; No. 2 will do the same in three minutes. We challenge any other Meat Cutters to do the same amount and same quality of work in so little time. We except none. Bell's is mad righ of right material, and acts accordingly. Interesting prices and catalogue free on request.

**BELL'S HAM PUMPS.** The best Ham Pumps ever invented. Used by the best packers all over the United States and Canada. Endorsed by all first-class houses. Does easier and better work than the imitations, lasts longer, and is sold as low as a first-class pump can be sold. Description, illustrations and prices for the asking.

Don't fail to write us. We are headquarters for Spiced Seasonings, Meat Cutters, Sausage Machinery, and other appliances. Tell us what you want and we'll tell you what we will do.

**THE WILLIAM G. BELL COMPANY,**

(Established 1861. Incorporated 1891.)     **BOSTON, MASS.**

## MEATS

The selection of these will naturally rest with the individual and will be governed by circumstances and the uses for which they are intended. All small pieces of wholesome meats, fat or lean, hearts, livers, cheek and weasand meat, which have small sale value in the market, may be made to yield good prices when worked up into sausages.

Certain kinds of beef offer opportunities for profit when employed as follows: By taking freshly killed beef while it is yet warm and chopping it up fine, while in this condition, it will absorb 50 per cent. or more of water. This is accomplished by adding water from time to time during the operation, taking care, however, to add no more water than is taken up by the meat itself. When prepared in this way it is necessary to allow the chopped mixture to properly cool off. It should not be immediately stuffed. It should be first spread in the refrigerator until it is cold, and thoroughly chilled. After this it is ready for spicing, manipulation and stuffing.

The beef from bulls furnishes the sausagemaker with a good and profitable meat for the making of bolognas and similar sausages. This meat being naturally of a dry nature will also absorb at least half its own weight of water, which may be added, as previously stated, during the process of chopping. This fact, although known by some experienced manufacturers, has always been considered as a valuable trade secret and may still be regarded as such. It is here publicly disclosed for the first time.

When slaughtered stags and boars can be more profitably made into sausages than they can be used for the customary cuts, judgment and discretion must be exercised so as not to use too large a proportion of this material. If too much is put in, a very poor and a faulty product is the result. In addition to this kind of sausage proving strong and unpalatable to the taste, the rank and disagreeable odor caused by their preparation for the table, will surely condemn the brand they bear, for any future consideration. Highly spicing or seasoning will not cover these disagreeable characteristics in this peculiar sausage. The only way to employ this meat is to use it in moderation.

It is advisable to have meat well chilled before chopping it; in this condition it cuts easier and better, not clogging the knives by becoming sticky. Before the meats and the fat are placed in the machine they should be cut into small pieces, about two or three inches square. This materially shortens the time required for reducing them to the required degree of fineness. When materials are to be chopped fine, no misgiving need arise that they can be made too fine. The finer the better, and the sausage therefrom will fully meet the requirements of the best trade.

For cutting fat into small squares or dice, special machines—fat cutters—are employed. Here, as with meat, it is also desirable to reduce the large pieces of fat to a convenient size before placing them in the machine.

Soft, oily fats should not be used where the large pieces or dice are to be employed, as a moderate temperature quickly softens such material, causing the oil to flow from it, thus giving a very unsightly appearance to the whole article. Such a sausage finds a poor sale and a low price. Back fat is best and cheapest in the end. This, containing a large amount of stearine, holds together and keeps its shape even in hot weather. It also helps to give the sausage a firm body, which soft and sloppy fat will not do.

This latter may be used when the fat is to be in a fine condition, such as in pork sausages, etc.

No particular instructions need be given for the general selection of meats. Each maker must choose for himself such pieces and parts as the requirements and conditions of his trade make necessary. In some localities, a rich fat sausage is desired. In others, a dry, lean one only satisfies the demands. Each manufacturer must determine for himself the points he will follow in this matter. The chief thing to be observed is to use only good and fresh meat, and to keep that in a fresh condition.

It is always beneficial to keep stock in refrigeration until wanted for immediate use in working into sausages. The pernicious practice of allowing it to stand in a warm workroom, exposed to heat and steam for hours before it is needed, should be strictly guarded against. Chopped meat when placed in coolers for keeping, should always be spread out, to permit the thorough chilling of all parts of the meat. No matter how low the temperature of the cooler may be, small pieces, when closely packed in trucks or boxes will heat in the middle of the mass where the cold air cannot penetrate. If the cut-up meat must be kept in this way for some time, it should be occasionally overhauled and transferred to another receptacle to allow the heat generated by close packing to escape. This treatment prevents meats and also fats from becoming sticky and musty. Where spreading is impracticable, the use of baskets or small perforated boxes is recommended to hold such stock, as these readily allow blood-stained water to escape. This, if confined with the meat, gives it a very uninviting appearance, besides affording a fruitful source for early decomposition. Of all packinghouse products, blood, under ordinary conditions, most easily becomes putrid.

**Hamburger Konservirungs Salz**

USE 2 OUNCES FOR EVERY 100 POUNDS OF MEAT.

Write for Circulars.

**White Konservirungs Salz**

Keeps Chopped Meat and Fresh Sausage the same as if it were frozen.

PUT UP IN
1 KILO BOXES = (2 lbs., 3½ oz.), $1.50 PER KILO.

**Red Konservirungs Salz**

Colors, Cures and Preserves Bolognas, Frankfurters, Etc., Per Pound, 27 Cents.

**WOLF, SAYER & HELLER,** NEW YORK: 120 Pearl Street. CHICAGO: Fulton and Peoria Streets.

---

## You Can't Make Good Sausage Without Good Pork and Beef!

BUY YOUR MEAT OF THE

# SCHWARZSCHILD & SULZBERGER CO.,

ESTABLISHED 1860.

New York—**ABATTOIRS**—Kansas City

Packers and Curers of Choicest Grades of Beef, Veal, Mutton and Pork. All Packinghouse Products.

MAIN OFFICES: 45th Street and First Avenue, New York.

ALSO, BRANCHES AND DEPOTS IN ALL THE PRINCIPAL CITIES IN THE U. S.

## The National Provisioner
### Analytical Laboratory

*Makes a specialty of furnishing information on the Utilization of all By-Products.*

*We can tell you how to get the most money out of your Greases, Tallows, etc.*

*We also make a specialty of the Examination for the Purity of all Ingredients used in the Manufacture of Sausages.*

*We can furnish you with Reliable Bleaching Processes. Write for prices.*

**The National Provisioner Analytical Laboratory,**

Official Chemists to the New York Produce Exchange.

150 NASSAU STREET, NEW YORK.

# IV

# BLOOD COLORS

## BLOOD COLORS

Any article in order to be salable must not only be satisfying to the taste but pleasing to the eye. This fact has caused manufacturers to vie with each other in the attractiveness of the package containing the goods as well as in the goods themselves. In certain departments of the packing industry, artificial coloring matters have contributed largely to giving the goods an attractive appearance. This is especially true of the sausage department. The trade now insists upon having sausages of a color not otherwise obtainable than by the use of artificial coloring matter.

In the course of their preparation, and through exposure to air, fresh meats lose, to a large extent, their bright color. The fresh appearance of meats in the sausage is a most desirable feature. To produce this effect, various substances are mixed with the sausage mass. These are known under the generic name, blood-color. These colors have as their basis harmless dyes or coloring matters obtained from various mineral and vegetable sources. With these dyes, other materials are intimately mixed or are impregnated and constitute what is known as dry blood-color. This may be procured in liquid form, also; so prepared that the necessary amount can be added directly, without further manipulation, to the sausage mass. The dry color must be dissolved in water previous to its use in coloring the sausage mixture.

From the standpoint of economy, when supplies are obtained from a distance, it is advisable to purchase blood color in the dry form and thus save transportation charges on an amount of water which can be added when needed for use, at the factory. There are times, however, when the convenient form of the liquid color, prepared and ready for immediate use, is a great convenience and saves the time and the trouble of preparing a solution.

In making the solution from the dry form of blood-color, particular care should be given to ensure the complete solubility of it. If the color is used in the sausage mass with particles remaining undissolved, these will appear in the finished sausage as bright red spots, giving the meat a very unnatural appearance.

When difficulty is experienced in obtaining a perfect solution from dry blood color, the solid particles should be allowed to settle and the clear, dissolved part poured off carefully into another vessel. More water should then be added to the residue and the whole well shaken or stirred; when the substance yields no more color to the water, the part remaining should be rejected and thrown away.

Many objections have been urged against the use of these artificial coloring matters, on the improper supposition that they are a menace to health. As a rule, these materials are not as injurious as general opinion would have them. Because of their great coloring power, extremely small quantities are used in sausages. As only the minute quantities necessary to produce the desired color are employed, there is every assurance that, so used, they are innocent ingredients.

The claim is made for some of these blood colors by their manufacturers that they are of vegetable origin; they also guarantee them absolutely harmless.

# Illinois Casing Company

EXPORTERS AND IMPORTERS

..OF..

# Sausage Casings

CHICAGO, ILL., U. S. A.

---

*Cable Address: "Commerce, Chicago."*

THIS BOOK will reach hundreds of Live Up-to-Date Sausagemakers who are large users of Machinery.

It's too late now for you to reach these people through an Announcement in this Authentic and Reliable Work, but you can do the next best thing by telling of the merits of your Machinery in the

## Advertising Columns Of.... The National Provisioner

The ORGAN of the Meat and Provision Industries of the United States.

There are very few Sausagemakers and Packers who will receive this book on the MANUFACTURE OF SAUSAGES who are not already subscribers to THE NATIONAL PROVISIONER. An excellent medium. It brings buyer and seller together.

**A SAMPLE COPY FOR THE ASKING.**

THE NATIONAL PROVISIONER PUBLISHING CO.,

150 Nassau Street, New York.

# V

# CASINGS

## CASINGS

Casings are made from the intestines of cattle, hogs and sheep. The weight and size of the bullock makes no particular difference in the quality of the casing. The best hog casings are obtained from hogs weighing from 125 to 300 pounds. Small hogs give narrow casings, which are not so advantageous as those from medium weight animals. Casings from young sheep cannot be used. Likewise, no casings are made from the entrails of calves.

The preparation and cleaning of casings require particular care, but those who make a business of this do it well. There is nothing which can be cleaner than a well prepared casing.

A great many casings are imported from various countries and they enjoy a good reputation. As a general rule, however, there are none better than those made in our own country, of which many pounds and sets are annually exported.

The method generally followed of preparing casings in this country is carried out very thoroughly and systematically. Machines for cleaning hog and beef casings are in use where there are large quantities to be handled. These machines do the work better than it can be done by hand and in very much less time, thus demonstrating their value as economical factors. Some, however, have objections to machine-cleaned and will use none but hand-cleaned casings. The latter are prepared in the following manner: The intestines coming from the animal are thoroughly flushed out with clean water to remove any refuse and undigested food. Then the surplus fat is at once removed from the outside by shaving with a sharp knife. After "fatting" they are then put in a tub or vat of warm water, washed, and scraped with a piece of wood, sharpened after the manner of a knife. By this means, the soft, mucous-like outside coating is removed. They are then turned inside out and the inside subjected to the same treatment. After the first scraping the casings are washed again and the scraping repeated. They are then well rinsed in cold water, drained and salted. Thereafter the casings are well rubbed with salt and packed in bunches or bundles for a few days. This treatment cures them and also gives them a chance to drain. The bunches, after remaining a sufficient time, are overhauled and the surplus salt shaken out. They are then re-rubbed with fine pulverized salt. This is known as "casing salt" and is specially made for this purpose.

When ready for shipment, they are packed in tight barrels or kegs, which are usually lined with cheese-cloth or muslin. Casings are sold by the piece, pound, or set. Each bunch or bundle will weigh, when packed, about four pounds, but this will vary. Casings are classed as hog bungs, and hog casings, beef bungs, rounds, and middles, sheep casings, and beef weasands; the latter, a lining from the throat of the bullock. Weasands are used as coverings for certain kinds of expensive sausages—chicken, ham, some kinds of tongue, etc.

Hog casings before being worked are generally soaked for two days; the first day in cold water, the next in warm pickle to bleach them and to induce fermentation, which makes them better and easier to work. In cleaning hog casings by hand, the back of a knife blade is used for scraping off the outside coatings.

Sheep intestines are soaked for three days before being cleaned. This course is necessary to toughen them sufficiently to allow their being handled without too many breakages. When ready for cleaning they are placed on an inclined board sloping to a tub of warm water and worked with the back edge of the knife until thoroughly clean and free from their slimy, soft surface.

Where the cleaning of casings is carried on it is important to bear in mind the necessity for a plentiful use of water for cleanliness. The scrapings from the casings and other refuse should be tanked or otherwise disposed of immediately after the work is done. The best place for this offal is in the grease rendering tank where any fat or grease can be recovered by the usual cooking. Where slaughtering is carried on in connection with the plant, this refuse from casings is tanked with the livers, lungs and other materials of this description. The accumulations of the cleaning room should not be allowed to lie around, as they contain enough filth in themselves to, in a short time, generate a very foul and disgusting odor.

### COLORING CASINGS

As trade demands require an attractive and presentable article, it has grown to be a legitimate practice to color the casings of sausages intended to be smoked. This is accomplished by soaking the prepared casings in a solution of the dye or other coloring material to be used, until the desired shade of color is obtained. Sausages stuffed in such casings take less time in smoking, and present a very rich appearance. Many dyes and "smoke colors" are on the market. By the use of some, it is claimed that no smoking of the sausage is required. But the better method of smoking for a shorter or longer time will always give more satisfactory results, and this method probably, will never be entirely superseded.

### A COLOR FOR CASINGS

A yellow color for staining or painting casings may be prepared by taking the coloring matter dissolved from three and a half ounces of saffron in about two quarts of water, to which has been added half a pint of alcohol. The yolks of eight or ten fresh eggs well beaten up in half a pint of water should also be added to the strained saffron solution. In summer no eggs need be used. The above color is applied to the hot sausages, but, previous to its application, the casings must be wiped clean of any grease boiled out while cooking. This color is very serviceable for Frankfort yellow sausage.

# VI

# STUFFING

## STUFFING

While stuffing, avoid putting too much material in the casing, and, on the other hand, stuff sufficiently to ensure a well-filled and rounded sausage. If the casing is not filled with the necessary amount of mass, while apparently full and firm, the sausage will soon shrink and present the shriveled appearance which, to most consumers is an unfailing sign of age. On the other hand, if there is too much material forced into the casing, the sausage, while presenting a handsome and firm appearance, will inevitably split and crack open in boiling or smoking. There is also danger of splitting or bursting the casing while stuffing, if attempts are made to stuff it to excess. A very little experience on the part of the operator soon enables him to ascertain the proper amount to put into each casing.

Sausages which are to be air dried are necessarily very firmly stuffed, to allow for the subsequent shrinkage caused by evaporation of the moisture within.

Previous to stuffing the sausage-meat into casings, they should be very flexible and wholly free from the salt in which they may have been packed. If this salt has not been thoroughly removed, the casing is not uniformly elastic and is liable to split during the operation of stuffing. If casings become too old it is poor economy to use them, as they will not stuff without many breakages, causing both loss and annoyance.

Casings are made to slip on the stuffing machine easily and are rendered very flexible by soaking them in slightly warm water for an hour or two before using. A pinch of bicarbonate of soda added to this water is often a material aid in softening them.

After filling large bolognas or any other sausages

which are stuffed into large casings, to prevent air bubbles which may be caught in these, from remaining, prick the sausages with a sharp, fine awl or similar instrument. Several sharpened thin wire nails, grouped together on a small piece of wood with a handle, make a serviceable plunger for this purpose.

Both hand and steam stuffers are employed. They are made in various sizes to suit the requirements of trade. Where large quantities of material are to be handled, automatic steam stuffers are always essential to profitable and economical working of the factory.

# VII

# COOKING

### ❦❦❦ THE LEADING HOUSE! ❦❦❦

## H. W<sup>M.</sup> DOPP & SON,

OLD No. 462
NEW No. 522 **Ellicott Street,**

Buffalo, N. Y., U. S. A.

MANUFACTURERS OF

**Seamless, Steam Jacketed Cast-Iron Kettles, Lard Mixers, Dryer and Cooler, Steam Jacketed Vacuum Pans, Etc.**

Complete Line of Soapmakers' Machinery.

DESCRIPTIVE CATALOGUE ON APPLICATION.

Lard Dryer, Mixer and Cooler.

Steam Jacketed Kettle.

---

## THE Silent Meat Cutters
### FOR SAUSAGE

**2450 MACHINES SOLD.**

Send For Catalogue.

## P. BILLINGHAM & CO.,
TRENTON, N. J.

---

# *Hand-Book and Directory*

## FOR PORK AND BEEF PACKERS

The subjects relating to all departments of the Packinghouse are fully covered in this book, giving the latest and most improved methods of successful packers, superintendents and foremen.

The Directory contains 7,000 names of the leading members of the wholesale trade, including Provision Brokers and Commission Merchants, Cottonseed Oil Manufacturers and Refiners, Fertilizer Manufacturers and Dealers, Soap and Candle Makers, etc.

*Price, $10.00.     Send for Circular.*

*The National Provisioner Publishing Company,*

150 NASSAU STREET, NEW YORK.

## COOKING

Sausages are preferably, and almost always, cooked in water-jacketed kettles, having steam and water connections for regulating the temperature. These kettles having a double shell extending around the bottom, sides and ends allow the water to circulate through this space, thus ensuring an equal distribution of heat throughout the contents of the kettle. With these a uniformly cooked sausage is obtained. Kettles of this description may be obtained in different forms and sizes with capacities of fifty gallons and upward.

The time required for cooking sausages varies with their nature. Specific instructions for each kind will be found in the recipes.

The fat and grease which boils out of sausages while cooking, should be carefully skimmed off and saved. If not impregnated too strongly with the spice odors, small portions may be added from time to time to rendered lard. If the skimmings should, however, be too highly spiced or aromatic, their proper place is in with the grease.

Skimmed grease from the cooking vat or kettle has always more or less water removed with it. This mixed water and grease should be separated at the earliest possible moment, for when they remain in this condition even for a very short time, the mixture becomes sour or fermented, thus destroying the availability of the grease for lard. If not convenient to separate this at once, the mixture may be held in good condition for a limited period by keeping it hot; but the sooner separated, the better will be the condition of the grease.

To bleach this grease to make it suitable for a white lard, the following formula has been found serviceable: For each 350 pounds of grease, boil up with it a mixture, dissolved in water, of borax, 3 oz.; sal-ammoniac, 1½ oz., and sal-soda, 9 oz. The whole is then cooked with open steam in a suitable tank or vessel for about 2 hours, after which time it is allowed to settle, when the bleached and whitened grease should be removed from the underlying liquid.

# VIII

# SMOKING

## SMOKING

THE dimensions of the smoke-house and the general arrangements desired must be determined by the business requirements.

A few points for obtaining the best results may be mentioned. The area of the smoking compartment should not be too large. If much material is to be smoked it is far better to divide the goods between two or three smaller houses, where the final results will justify this procedure. There is less shrinkage in a house four feet wide than in one three or four times as large, and a small house also smokes out quicker. The trouble with a wide house is that the wind shifts the smoke from one side to the other and one portion of the house may have its smoking finished, while another side has hardly been affected.

The best materials for producing the smoke are hard woods like hickory and maple. Hard wood sawdust makes a good smudge and it may be economically employed. Pine or any resinous wood is never used for smoking. A small quantity of juniper berries is sometimes burned with smouldering sawdust fires, for the purpose of imparting flavor to certain kinds of sausages.

When it is required to smoke sausages, they are hung a short distance apart on the sticks by the looped string. These sticks should be made to fit across a section of the smoke-house, wherein they are placed with the hanging sausages. This method greatly facilitates the handling. Where large quantities of sausages are to be smoked, a framework of iron can be used for holding the sticks of sausages. This frame can be built so that it will fit the smoke-house or a section of it, and be suspended from an overhead iron track which extends from inside the smoke-house to any desired distance outside. This frame can be filled outside of the house and then run within, on the track. Thus it will be necessary to open the doors but once, to place a large amount of sausages in smoke. After being sufficiently smoked, the framework, full of sausages, may be as rapidly removed and run on the track to any desired place in the factory where it can be unloaded when convenient. By this method of rapid placing and withdrawal, the temperature of the smoke-house is not affected or at most, to a very slight degree. This is a very efficient means for keeping an even temperature while filling and emptying the smoke-house.

In placing the sausages on the wooden sticks, care must be taken to avoid the crowding of too many sausages on any one stick; and also when placing the full sticks in the smoke-house, care should be exercised to avoid overlapping the tiers. If this is not done the sausages will be streaked or spotted, and, overcrowding the sticks, will further prevent the sausages from being evenly smoked.

The drafts of the smoke-house should receive careful attention to ensure good results while smoking the stock. When starting the fires after a house is filled, the ventilators at the top and at the bottom should be kept open for a while. After the fires are well under way, the ventilators must be closed, the drafts regulated, and the fires banked with hardwood sawdust. Great care should be taken, especially in warm weather, to see that the fires are well banked, so that they cannot burn freely and thus create unnecessary heat. Too high a temperature should never be allowed during the smoking process as it will cause a large shrinkage in the stock.

When it is desired to produce a cold smoke, a low smouldering fire should be kept up and the sausages hung as far away as practicable from it, to, at the same time, obtain the benefit of the smoke. A method sometimes employed for "cold smoking," is to build the fire some distance from the smoke-house and convey the smoke thence underneath the surface, so that part of the heat may escape at the fire and the remainder of it on the way to the house, where the smoke, deprived of all the heat, is utilized.

### COATING AFTER SMOKING

In hot weather, or where smoked sausages are to be shipped long distances, they should have a protective coating applied to the casings, by dipping the finished hot sausage in the prepared compound. This will prevent them becoming mouldy even when hung in a damp cooler. It also preserves their plump appearance as well as precludes sweating and shrinkage.

The coating should be of such a nature as will permit its easy removal by simply wiping the sausages with a soft cloth, after which they will have a bright and clean appearance. The expense of applying such a coating is insignificant as compared with the saving in shrinkage it effects, and the ability to subsequently hang or store the sausages in almost any place.

# IX

# FILLERS

## FILLERS

Many kinds of sausage have added to them filling material intimately mixed with the meats and spices. The addition of these different food materials is not only desirable but even necessary at times, for various and obvious reasons. They cheapen the cost of the meats employed for sausage manufacture, and, at the same time, substantially improve the looks of the sausage by giving it compactness and a firm body. Moisture is also retained by their use, which is a desirable and important feature, as the more moisture is carried, the more the saving in the weight of the meat employed. Considering only the cost of the meats and of the labor necessary for their production, without these filling materials, it would often be an unprofitable undertaking to make and sell sausages for the prices frequently obtained.

The materials commonly used for this purpose are bread, corn-starch, potato and other kinds of flour, cracker and sausage meal and boiled rice. Other substances may be added as fillers but those mentioned are in general use by most sausagemakers. Not all of these are added at the same time nor to the same sausage, but usually, one or two as occasion requires. For example, in bolognas, potato flour only may be used. In pork sausage, cracker meal, or cracker or sausage meal together may be added. The method of utilizing these various ingredients will be described in the recipes given for the manufacture of each class of sausage.

In some classes of sausages, such as summer sausage, salami, etc., no water, and, consequently, no fillers, as potato flour, sausage meal and like material are added in the manufacture of these "dry" sausages. The aim is to have the least possible moisture encased with the material, in order to aid in the period of ripening, and also to avoid the appearance of the skins or casings being only half stuffed after drying out. Cool, dry storage is necessary for this class of goods.

Should these sausages, in the process of "ripening," through unsuitable storage become mouldy, remove this mould by washing them in a solution of alum, and, after draining, wipe with a cloth saturated with lard or cottonseed oil.

These sausages—summer, cervelat, salami, etc.,—necessarily command a high price, being, in a way, condensed matter and devoid of the usual amount of moisture and fillers. They are not intended for immediate sale when manufactured, as is the case with the great bulk of sausages.

Any kind of lean meats may be used for making summer sausages, and as such, will probably bring a larger profit than when used in any other way. There is an ever increasing demand for this class of sausage, and even though the present output is large and constantly increasing, the demand more than exceeds the supply.

Unquestionably the best disposition of small pieces of meats, when such are difficult to profitably dispose of otherwise, is to use them for the manufacture of summer sausages.

SAUSAGE MEAL is an excellent ingredient as a filler, combining most of the useful properties of all the others. It is especially prepared with this end in view; but there are occasions when this may be better replaced by some of the other fillers used in certain classes of goods. One advantage this meal possesses over bread and boiled rice is that it can be added directly to the sausage mass without any previous preparation. It holds moisture well, absorbs the free oily fat and imparts good flavor to the sausage.

CRACKER MEAL is not used to the extent that its superior characteristics would seem to warrant. The addition of a small amount of this to pork sausages gives a very superior article. Not only does it give a desirable taste and flavor, but also causes it to become nicely browned and crisp, having an appetizing appearance when prepared for the table. Its use in this sausage is highly recommended and the satisfaction resulting from its employment is certainly an advantage not to be lightly considered. This meal is made on a small scale by taking common crackers and rolling them with a crusher on a board until the required degree of fineness is obtained. The finer the meal can be made the better it is for this purpose.

BREAD is an important and inexpensive article for filling in sausages. It is allowed to become stale or partly dried out, as in this condition it can be used with better effect than in its fresh state. Bakers' bread is more advantageously used than the home made article, as the former will absorb much more water and, ordinarily, is of a much lighter texture. If the crust of the bread is charred or burned, it should first be removed before preparing it for mixing purposes, as its dark color will appear in the sausage and injure the bright apearance necessary for an attractive, inviting article. The bread, freed from all objectionable features, is thoroughly soaked in water to a uniform consistency (which may require several hours). It is afterwards pressed well to remove the excess of water. While still moist, it is broken into small fragments by working with the hands until the pressed mass is in a comparatively uniform state; then it is placed in the mixing machine with the other ingredients of the sausage. This material is very serviceable in reducing the cost without detracting in the least from the nutritive qualities of the sausage as a whole.

Boiled Rice gives firmness and fullness to the sausage and is a good adhesive material for holding the mixture together. It retains its moisture for a long time, preventing the shriveled appearance commonly observed in some carelessly prepared products. A precaution to be observed while using this material is to allow the boiled rice to become thoroughly cold before mixing it with the other stock; otherwise it will have a very decided tendency to become sour, communicating this sourness to the other materials, thus spoiling the whole mass.

Potato Flour and common flour act also as filling materials for the mixtures and carry a very large percentage of moisture, giving the sausage good weight and a plump appearance. These flours are excellent filling materials and serve to the fullest extent the use for which they are intended. In adding common flour to mixtures, it is first made into a smooth paste free from lumps. In this condition it is gradually worked in with the meat and other materials.

Corn Starch is sometimes used, as is also rye flour but their employment is not very extensive.

The object of all these materials, as previously stated, is to cheapen the cost of the sausage by carrying in it a large amount of water.

A Substitute for Starch. An excellent filler for sausages is pounded veal, which is prepared as follows: From a very heavy calf take the still warm ham immediately after killing. Cut out as quickly as possible most of the sinews and fat, and cut the lean meat into flat pieces about the size of the hand. Then speedily pound these meat pieces with a wooden mallet on a smooth block. In cold weather the pounded pieces are to be heaped up in the middle of the block and covered with a cloth. The whole heap is then pounded again, the operator moving slowly around the block all the while. Repeat this heaping and pounding until the whole mass is fine and of a gluish consistency. A little salt should be added from time to time while pounding.

This operation has to be done quickly and all help at disposal should be called into requisition at this juncture, as it is very essential that the meat should not become cold while being pounded. The mass should now be further chopped for ten minutes, keeping the knife blades wet. Water is then added in the proportion of one gallon for every ten pounds of meat and, afterwards, another quart for the same weight. To the mixture must also be added 8¾ oz. of salt, three-quarters of an ounce of cane sugar and three-eighths ounce powdered saltpetre. The whole mass should now be well kneaded for 10 minutes and until it becomes quite solid and viscous. Now place the pounded veal in another vessel, in layers about 2 inches thick and allow it to remain there for 10 or 12 hours; the mass of this will have a fine red color. The above filler is used according to the consistency desired for the sausage mass. To every 10 lbs. of the meat mass, 2 lbs. of this substitute may be added. Before incorporating it with the sausage mixture, the pounded meat should be rubbed up with some water. Like other fillers, it must be well incorporated with the sausage ingredients.

This meat is very suitable for Ham Sausage, Mortadelli Meat, Vienna and Knack Sausages, Press-Cheese and in general, for all sausages which are smoked and immediately scalded. Every sausage prepared from this compound will get stiff when cooked and slice well when cold. It is also possible to use bull or cow meat from the round for making this substitute, but it will be much inferior to that prepared from the veal and it will not absorb so much water. The quicker the work is done and the longer the natural heat of the meat is retained before being worked, the better will be the product obtained. In smoking sausages containing this filler, a few handfuls of juniper berries added to the smouldering fire gives them a finer flavor.

# X

# PRESERVATIVES

NEW YORK and - - CHICAGO.

To Make Good Sausage, Use

## WOLF, SAYER & HELLER'S
### Best Spice

**NOTHING LIKE IT**     **SEND TRIAL ORDER**

|  | Bbls. | Price Half Bbl. | 25, 50 and 100 lbs. |
|---|---|---|---|
| P SPICE for Pork Sausage, | 14c | 15c | 16c |
| B SPICE for Bologna and Smoked Sausage, | 14c | 15c | 16c |
| F SPICE for Frankfort and Wiener Wurst, | 14c | 15c | 16c |
| L SPICE for Liver, Blood Sausage and Head Cheese, | 14c | 15c | 16c |
| C SPICE for Celery Pork Sausage, | 22c | 23c | 25c |

120 Pearl Street, New York.    Fulton and Peoria Streets, Chicago.

# THE YELLOW BOOK

### A Book on the Manufacture of... Cottonseed Oil

And allied products, containing facts in regard to the fundamental principles of the treatment of cottonseed in relation to COTTONSEED MEAL and COTTONSEED OIL. Valuable hints about the practical manufacture of some of the latest methods for refining, cake analysis, butterine and margarine. A list of Cottonseed Oil Mills in the United States. Price, $3.00 per copy.

**SEND FOR CIRCULAR**

### The National Provisioner Publishing Company,

150 NASSAU STREET, NEW YORK.

---

## Books!

If there is ANY book you want, on ANY subject, it would be to your advantage to communicate with us. It would save you trouble and expense

### The National Provisioner Publishing Co.,

BOOK DEPARTMENT     150 NASSAU STREET, NEW YORK.

# PRESERVATIVES

These may be divided into three general classes:

- Cold Storage or Refrigeration.
- Salt.
- Chemicals.

## COLD STORAGE OR REFRIGERATION

The first and best preservative is cold storage. This is applicable for keeping almost indefinitely food products when the proper and necessary conditions are observed. Among these conditions is a dry cold atmosphere and the absence of any notable amount of moisture or dampness. When humidity is present in a marked degree the conditions are ripe for the formation of mould, which under these favorable conditions rapidly grows upon all animal and vegetable matter, rendering such articles more or less unsightly. Excessive moisture should be removed from the air as much as possible by placing in convenient corners of the cold storage rooms receptacles, filled with ordinary quick-lime. This, after having absorbed all the moisture it will, can be cheaply and quickly replaced with fresh quantities of lime.

A better, but perhaps a little more expensive agent for this purpose, is fused chloride of calcium, a material extensively used in the cold storage of fruit as a necessary protection against the accumulation of moisture. Chloride of calcium absorbs moisture from the surrounding air with great rapidity, keeps the atmosphere in the room perfectly dry and lasts a long time.

With many butchers and small meat dealers natural ice is largely replaced for refrigerating purposes by small, compact and efficient ice-making machines. These are so much more economical in regard to the space occupied and to the expense of producing the required amount of refrigeration, that it seems only a question of time when they will entirely supersede natural ice for this purpose. These facts may be appreciated most thoroughly by those depending upon outside sources for their supply of ice.

A small ice-making machine is a leading feature in the modern, well-equipped sausage factory. Where any considerable quantities of sausages and meats are handled, the small ice machine is not only a convenience, but a necessity. The advantage it offers over the old-fashioned way of storing ice is alone sufficient to commend its use. When its work is accomplished by producing the required temperature, the machine is stopped, and the expense of running it then ceases. It is a much more cleanly method of obtaining refrigeration, and, as before mentioned, is much more simple and economical. Before planning the erection or extensive repairs of ice-houses or boxes, the merits of these machines should be investigated, when the fact of their superior merit will undoubtedly be made apparent. These ice-making machines are constructed with capacities varying from half a ton to 400 tons daily. Essential as is mechanical refrigeration to the large packer, it is no less so to the smaller packer and the butcher who wish to successfully compete with others in this era of close working and small profit.

The temperature of the place chosen for cold storage is a most important consideration. It should be as carefully regulated as possible and no wide variations allowed from the degree of cold necessary for the proper preservation of the substances placed therein.

## SALT.

Salt has been for ages and is to-day universally employed as a preservative. It is used in the meat industry for the seasoning, curing and packing of all kinds of meats, preventing decomposition by absorbing moisture from the flesh and tissues, and at the same time imparting a flavor which is not possible with any other agent. Not only is it invaluable as an antiseptic, but it has the advantage of being also a tonic, a certain amount being necessary for health. Used in its natural state or in solution, as in brine or pickle, it is an ideal preservative. Without the use of salt, there could not exist the vast packing industry which we have to-day. Its use in the dry-salt department, with the enormous range of the products dependent upon its curative properties, is sufficient evidence of its value as a dry agency and in its solution as a pickle. The absolute dependence upon salt alone, to preserve for future consumption, such unlimited quantities of perishable goods attests its unequaled importance as an antiseptic and a preservative.

Many kinds and varieties of salt are used. There is no difference in their composition, but they are characterized by the size and the different forms of the grains or crystals and the source of their origin.

With this ingredient, as with the other materials used in the manufacture of sausages, selection of the proper kinds should be made. Ordinary salt generally contains insoluble matter, such as dirt and sand and usually, more or less of lime and magnesia salts in the form of sulphates and chlorides. Some of these impurities impart a bitter taste to the meats and other materials in connection with which such salt is used.

All salt selected should be as free from impurities as possible, with a view to its general qualifications and its fitness for the use to which it may be placed.

## CHEMICALS

The use of antiseptics for the preservation of meats and sausages has come to be recognized as legitimate and even necessary. Among those commonly used are

Borax, Boracic Acid, Preservaline and other preservatives more or less effective. These preservatives have their legitimate functions, as unquestionably much good and valuable food would be lost and wasted, especially in the hot summer months, if there were no easy and convenient means for preserving it against decomposition.

The trouble lies in the fact that when there is a legitimate use in moderate quantities of such articles, abuses creep in which arouse antagonism and agitate the question of their entire prohibition; but those who use preservatives intelligently and in moderate quantities will always have beneficial results and need not fear any harmful effects therefrom. A good maxim to remember is: Don't use 2 oz. when 1 oz. will do the work.

Saltpetre, or, chemically speaking, potassium nitrate, is of great value because it imparts the peculiar and desired natural ruddy color to meats, whether cured in dry salt or pickle. Without its assistance it would be almost impossible to prepare meats to suit many markets.

To obtain this desired natural color it is necessary to use only 4 oz. of saltpetre to 100 pounds of meat. If too much saltpetre is used it will have a tendency to cause the meat to have a shriveled appearance.

Other preparations classed as preservatives are also used. Many of these are compounded from formaldehyde and salts of antiseptic capability. The same may be said of these as of the soda salts; used in the quantities necessary to accomplish their purposes it is doubtful if any of these are harmful to the health of the individual.

Especial care, however, should be observed in using all preservatives, adhering strictly to the prescribed methods of use and the quantities involved, rejecting, absolutely, the idea that if a little is good, more is better.

Salicylic acid has also certain antiseptic qualities, and it is employed as a preservative, but its use at the present time is not very general as a preservative for sausages. It has been conclusively shown by a carefully conducted series of experiments, that salicylic acid exerts a decided influence in retarding digestion, as small a quantity as two hundredths of one per cent. showing this detrimental effect. We cannot recommend the use of salicylic acid because of the liability to use in harmful quantities.

---

Owing to the general tendency of antiseptics to prevent drying out, it has been found most satisfactory in the manufacture of summer or "dry" sausages of this class, to dispense with them altogether. Under their action it is almost impossible to "ripen" goods, so treated. The large amount of moisture removed in the curing, together with the salt added to season them, is sufficient to hold them for a long period without the use of any preservative.

# THE MURRAY IRON WORKS CO.,

BURLINGTON, IOWA, U. S. A.

Leading Manufacturers of Machinery for Butchers, Packers and Sausagemakers.

**Choppers, Cutters, Rockers,**
  **Steam Stuffers, Mixers,**
    **Rendering Apparatus,**
      **Tanks, Kettles, Coolers,**
**Fertilizer Dryers,**
  **Steam Engines and Boilers,**
    **Ice and Refrigerating Machinery.**

CATALOGUES FREE ON APPLICATION.

---

# THE BROWN BOOK

Is welcomed by all...

## GLUE AND GELATINE MANUFACTURERS

It is a practical treatise on the Manufacture of Glue and Gelatine. A book which no one engaged in this line of business can afford to be without. Everything in regard to the manufacture of Glue and Gelatine is exhaustively treated.

**The price is $10 per copy.**

SEND FOR CIRCULAR.

**THE NATIONAL PROVISIONER PUBLISHING COMPANY,**

150 Nassau Street, New York.

# XI

# GENERAL INFORMATION

## GENERAL INFORMATION.

SCALES.—It is seldom that the scales in the average factory receive the attention and care they should. It is too often taken for granted that they are always correct. With unreliable or faulty scales, it is a very easy matter to suffer great losses by unknowingly giving overweight in sales. A scale weighing light occasions much trouble and annoyance, and lays the seller open to the suspicion of dishonest dealing. Serious consequences are avoided by having all the scales periodically examined and overhauled and also very frequently tested by standard weights. The steam and large amount of moisture usually present in every sausage factory, constantly enveloping the scales, have a tendency to rust their bearings, thereby causing these to work stiffly. This accumulation of rust, if not removed, soon impairs the accuracy of all scales.

The steel bearings of all platform scales exposed to the action of water or brine, should have an impervious coating applied to them. This should be painted on sufficiently thin to allow the usual free working of these parts. A small outlay for occasional overhauling will prove in the end to be a profitable investment.

POUNDING MEATS.—A useful article for pounding meats is a mallet made of beech wood 9 inches long and 5 inches square, with a 16-inch handle. This sized mallet is very serviceable in making the substitute for starch.

REMOVING TRIMMINGS.—A necessary appliance for removing closely packed trimmings is a pitchfork. When trimmings are closely packed in barrels and stored for some time, they become almost a solid mass, which can only be separated and removed with difficulty. The ordinary light-tined fork is very frequently broken in taking these from the barrels. A pitchfork which will stand almost any severe usage in this connection is made of heavy steel, with teeth an inch thick at the base and three-quarters of an inch wide, tapering to a point. The shank of the fork is made of heavy steel, giving rigidity and strength to the tool as a whole.

MACHINERY.—Another article often used in the cylinders of stuffing machines is a flexible plug made from the shoulder hide of an old boar or stag. This yielding, and more or less elastic plug is made from a hide 2 to 3 inches thick and formed to fit the cylinder snugly. It will remedy whatever imperfections there may be in the cylinders of old machines.

MANAGEMENT.—It is of the utmost importance that a systematic detailed account be kept of every item connected with the business. While individual methods may vary, there are some general principles common to all. Any plan to be of business value must necessarily take note of every item of expense in connection with the production of any article. Materials, wages, clerks' and office expenses, shipping expenses, packages, rent, taxes, deterioration of plant, repairs to factory and machinery, light, heat and power, advertising, printing, stationery, postage, etc., are among the items to be considered in ascertaining the cost of manufacture.

Further account must be taken of shrinkage, loss on returned goods, exchanges, experiments, bad debts, etc.

These several items may be grouped under three general heads: The first, to include the purchase of raw materials and all articles to be used in the factory; the second, to deal with the product made and the cost price of the same; the third, to cover the cost and fixed charges incidental to the sale of the manufactured goods.

With a system once arranged for noting these accounts, it is no trouble to keep a record of every detail of cost connected with the operation of the plant, and thus afford a safe guide as to the percentage of profit and loss upon the business.

The importance of adopting and thoroughly carrying out a well conceived system of arriving at the actual cost, is obvious.

Appended is a test made in one of the large western packinghouses on manufactured sausage; it shows how completely and accurately every detail was taken into account in arriving at the cost of producing the finished sausage, packed and ready for shipment. The test selected is taken at random from among many others.

### RING BOLOGNA SAUSAGE TEST

| | | | |
|---|---|---|---|
| 420 Lbs. | Beef Hearts | @ 1½c. per lb. | $6.30 |
| 180 " | Weasand Meat | @ 1c. " | 1.80 |
| 260 " | Corned Beef | @ 2c. " | 5.20 |
| 60 " | Corned Ox Lips | @ 1c. " | .60 |
| 373 " | Beef Head and Cheek Meat | @ 1⅞c. " | 6.99 |
| 60 " | Fat Pork Butts | @ 8¼c. " | 4.95 |
| 3¼ " | Black Pepper | @ 6½c. " | .21 |
| 1½ " | Allspice | @ 7c. " | .10 |
| 1⅛ " | Saltpetre | @ 4½c. " | .05 |
| 6 " | Potato Flour | @ 2c. " | .12 |
| 6 " | Borax | @ 8½c. " | .51 |
| 6 " | Coriander Seed | @ 6c. " | .36 |
| 12 Sets of Round Casings (beef). | | @ 12c. | 1.44 |
| 1¾ Lbs. Twine | | @ 31 c. " | .54 |
| Wood and Sawdust | | | .15 |
| 21 Lbs. Coating | | @ 5c. " | 1.05 |
| Total | | | $30.37 |

## RING BOLOGNA SAUSAGE TEST.

Less:
26 Lbs. Bologna Meat Returned by
   Stuffers ............... @ 3c. per lb. .78
16 " Corned Beef Trimmings .@ ½c. " .08
48 " Beef Head and Cheek Meat,@ 1c. " .48
 2 " Waste Casings......... @ ½c. " .01
                  $1.35

|  |  |  | Green Weight | Per Cent. |
|---|---|---|---|---|
| 1256 Lbs. | Meat Chopped, |  |  |  |
| 1310 " | Bologna |  |  |  |
| 1184 " | " | After Smoking | 90 | 37-100 |
| 1183 " | " | After Cooking | 90 | 30-100 |
| 1204 " | " | After Dipping | 91 | 91-100 |

Labor:
Two Men Trucking Meat to Sausage
 Dep't. .......................¾ hr. $1.75 $ .25
Two Men Making up Casings......¾ " 1.50 .22
Two Men Grinding...............⅓ " 1.75 .11
Trimmings 540 Lbs. ............. .10 .54
One Man Chopping ..............2 " 2.25 .45
Two Men Stuffing, 27c. per 1,000 lbs. Meat Chopped, .68
Two Men Tieing, 19c. " 1,000 lbs............. .47
Two Men Hanging, 13c. " 1,000 lbs............. .32
Four Men Trucking and Hanging
 into House ... ................⅓ hr. $1.50 $ .20
One Man Smoking...............½ " 2.00 .10
Three Men Trucking from Sausage
 House to Cook Tubs...........¼ " 1.50 .12
One Man Trucking from Cook
 Tubs to Packing Dep't. .........⅓ " 1.50 .05
One Man Cooking ..............¾ " 2.00 .15
Two Men Dipping................1 " 1.50 .30
                  $3.96

Cost per 100 Lbs. Packed Ready for Shipment:

| | | |
|---|---|---|
| Meat, Spices, etc. | $2.52 | 24-100 |
| Labor, Manufacturing | .32 | 89-100 |
| " Packing | .10 | |
| " Additional | .28 | |
| Nails | .00 | 42-100 |
| Veneering | .00 | 27-100 |
| Four 25-lb. Boxes | .34 | |
| Administrative Expenses | .25 | $3.82 82-100 |
| Less Offal | .11 | 11 21-100 |
| Net Cost | | 3.71 61-100 |

Cost Loose, $3.27 per 100 lbs. Sausage.
Cost Packed, $3.72 " " "

### AROMATIC BRINE

A brine which may be advantageously used in curing any kind of fancy meats, and also for hams, tongues, corned beef, bayonne hams, etc., is made in the following manner: To 8 gallons of water add 12 lbs. of salt. To 2 gallons of water boiled up for 5 minutes add 1 lb. of cane sugar, 7 oz. of pure saltpetre, 2¾ oz. of coriander seed, one-tenth ounce dry bay leaves and two pieces of garlic. The solution is then strained and added to the brine. During hot weather it is also necessary to add to it 2 ozs. of boracic acid for each ten gallons for preservative purposes.

# XII

# SAUSAGE RECIPES

To Make GOOD SAUSAGE Use

# WOLF, SAYER & HELLER'S

Extra Selected

SHEEP, HOG and BEEF **CASINGS**

ONE QUALITY.     THE BEST.

OWN MANUFACTURE.

Everything in Butchers', Packers' and Sausage-makers' Supplies.

120 Pearl Street, NEW YORK.     Fulton & Peoria Streets, CHICAGO.

**WRITE FOR CATALOGUE.**

---

**A Practical Work on the Manufacture of Linseed Oil and Varnishes is had in the Red Book**

Giving most valuable information in regard to the Manufacture and Treatment of LINSEED OIL in all its phases. The book carries the reader through the many complications that he meets in this business. These important facts have heretofore never been published. The MANUFACTURE OF VARNISHES is treated in such a way as to be thoroughly understood by all readers.

The Book is Essentially Practical In Every Detail......

Price, $5.00.

Send for Circular

---

**The National Provisioner Publishing Co.,**
150 NASSAU STREET, NEW YORK.

## SAUSAGE RECIPES

Recipes naturally vary in quantity of meat, fillers and amount of seasoning dependent upon the demands of the trade. Locality has much to do with this, and nationality more. In some sections cayenne pepper, garlic, etc., are absolutely necessary; in others, thyme, sage, marjoram, etc., while, again, a superabundance of salt is demanded; as before noted, these conditions must be met by the judgment of the individual manufacturer.

When lean trimmings are mentioned in recipes, it means the regular run of trimmings under normal conditions; not too much fat, yet not utterly devoid of it. A small portion of boracic acid is always beneficial and safe to use; in fresh stock 5 oz. per 100 lbs. is sufficient and 8 to 10 oz. in smoked stock.

Salt meats may often be employed to advantage in some kinds of sausages. When these are used, due allowance must be made in seasoning for the amount of salt the meat contains.

In some of the following recipes directions will be found for working the sausage mass by hand, by kneading on the block, etc. These directions can be readily adapted to the working by machinery where large quantities of material are to be handled. Many small dealers not having occasion to manufacture these sausages on the larger scale, will thus be enabled to carry out the formula by the method indicated.

Several recipes are given in which the seasoning is added by the weight in grains. To weigh off this small fraction in parts of an ounce to which this weight is equivalent would be inconvenient and troublesome. The scale for weighing spices is specially adapted for weighing these small quantities, and the advantage of such a fine scale is further demonstrated. A set of these grain weights can be purchased of the makers of these scales or of any dealer.

For those who may wish to get the equivalent of the grain weights in fractions of an ounce, by dividing the given number of grains into 438, the proportional part of the weight in ounces is obtained. For example, when 73 grains of spice are directed to be used, 73 divided into 438 gives 6; or, 73 grains is equivalent to one-sixth of an ounce.

Some sausages for which recipes are given in the following pages, have not hitherto been made in this country, owing to the difficulty of procuring reliable recipes for them. The recipes printed herein will enable the sausage-maker to manufacture sausages equal in every way to the fancy imported article which retails at a higher price.

### PORK SAUSAGE

Eighty pounds of nice, lean fresh pork trimmings, chopped fine; 16 lbs. well boiled rice, pulverized; 2 lbs. pigs liver, also chopped fine; and 2 lbs. unsmoked, nice, cured bacon are taken, and the whole well chopped and thoroughly mixed. To this may be added, if necessary, water to make the desired consistency. Season the above with 22 oz. fine salt, 6 oz. best ground white pepper, 1½ oz. fine cayenne pepper, 1 oz. ground nutmeg, 1 oz. ground cloves, 1 oz. ground mace, and a small quantity of finely powdered sage, if such flavor is desired. The mass must be thoroughly incorporated, as usual, with all sausage stock and seasoning. Stuff the mass in sheep casings, making very small links, if for fancy trade, and in small hog casings if for regular trade. The above is an excellent recipe, though to suit some tastes or particular trade the seasoning may have to be slightly altered; the above seasoning is rather high. If such sausage is to be shipped or kept over longer than usual, to the fresh stock add for each 100 lbs., 5 oz. powdered boracic acid, which will prevent decomposition (fermentation) and will in no way interfere with the sausage as regards flavor, etc.

This sausage mass is often put up in 2 or 3 pound white muslin bags and sold under various fancy names of sausage meat.

It is also sold by retailers as chopped sausage meat.

### PORK SAUSAGE—ANOTHER RECIPE

Use nice, lean pork trimmings, well chopped, and, to each 40 lbs. add 8 lbs. of well boiled rice and mix well. To this mixture add 1 lb. of the following seasoning: 4 oz. best white pepper, 1 oz. cayenne pepper and 1 lb. fine salt, well mixed. This makes a very fine pork sausage. Use hog casings for stuffing the mass. To the above, when desired, 1½ lbs. of cracker meal may be added, which will greatly improve the sausage. Sausage meal may also be added to the mass while chopping, in place of the cracker meal.

### PORK SAUSAGE—ANOTHER RECIPE

Take 75 lbs. of lean pork trimmings, 5 lbs. lean beef, 15 lbs. boiled rice or potato flour, and add to the chopped mass 3 quarts water; season with 24 oz. fine salt, 7 oz. white pepper, 2 oz. ground ginger, and a small quantity of sage if desired. Mix well, fill in hog casings and twist off into links of the usual size and style.

### SMOKED PORK SAUSAGE

Take 51 lbs. beef chuck meat, 25 lbs. salt pork trimmings, and 24 lbs. fresh pork trimmings to make 100 lbs. of stock. Chop and mix well, and season the mass with 4 oz. of borax, 18 oz. mace, 4 oz. cayenne pepper, and 8 oz. rubbed sage.

Treat the mass the same as usual for pork sausages, forming links, and after drying a short time smoke from one and a half to two hours.

The above seasoning may be too high for some trade, but it can be altered to suit the various conditions.

### OXFORD SAUSAGE

Take 6 lbs. lean and fat pork and 6 lbs. veal (free from skin). To this add 3 lbs. beef suet and 1 lb. of bread prepared as filler. Mix with the above 1 lb. cracker or sausage meal and the necessary quantity of blood color, if it is desired to use this. Chop the whole very fine. To the meats, add first the sausage or cracker meal, then the necessary amount of seasoning, and, finally, the blood color. Add sufficient salt to obtain the required flavor, stuff in hog or sheep casings, and make the usual links, as with pork sausage.

This sausage will meet the requirements of fancy trade.

### BEEF SAUSAGE

Take 12 lbs. of lean beef, 8 lbs. of fat, 4 lbs. of prepared and pressed bread, 4 lbs. of sausage meal, and 14 oz. of mixed seasoning and salt. Cut the beef and fat into 2 inch squares, mix in the bread and cut all moderately fine. Add the sausage meal dry, with water sufficient to moisten this and the other ingredients, and chop the whole very fine. Use either sheep casings or narrow hog casings for stuffing; or the mass may be retailed in the market as beef sausage meat.

### FRANKFORT PORK SAUSAGE

This is made of pork, ham, shoulder, and belly moderately fat. It is advisable to use best quality of meat, of good, firm consistency, from young, light hogs. If short of such meat, add one-third beef. First chop 100 lbs. pork to half a walnut size, add 10 oz. salt, a little water, and continue chopping until about the size of a pea. Add 5¼ oz. white pepper, 1 2-5 oz. mace, 15 pieces garlic and 10 shallots finely scraped. Chop to about corn size, break up the mass several times on the block without kneading. Fill into narrow salted beef casings of about 15 inches. Stuff firmly. Allow to dry 8 to 10 hours, smoke at about 65° F. until of a reddish yellow color and seethe in boiling water 25 or 30 minutes. No saltpetre should be used for this sausage. It is very delicious when hot.

### FRANKFORT SAUSAGE—ANOTHER RECIPE

Use 60 lbs. pork trimmings and 40 lbs. beef trimmings. To this add 1 lb. potato flour mixed with sufficient water to make the mass. When these are incorporated, of the requisite consistency, season with 8 oz. ground pepper, 4 oz. ground cardamom, 4 oz. allspice and salt to taste. Mix all the ingredients in the chopping machine and chop as fine as possible. Blood color may be added if desired. The mass is removed from the machine and kneaded by hand for half an hour, then stuffed into narrow casings. The sausages are smoked for about 30 minutes over a hot fire. They are then put in hot water, 160° F., for 3 to 5 minutes, taken out and placed in water until cold.

### VIENNA SAUSAGE (WIENERWURST)

According to the market price of meat, use one-half or one-third pork, the rest veal; two-thirds veal and one-third pork will make a delicate and tender sausage. For 100 lbs stock use:

Fifty pounds meat of young beef, not fat, from shoulder, neck or back; 50 lbs. fat pork from young, tender hogs. Each kind of meat is cut up separately into pieces of about bean size, mixed with the required amount of salt, saltpetre and sugar, and with about 5 pints of water put into the salt. It is now firmly pressed together and left at rest in an earthenware vessel; in winter in a heated, and in summer in a cool room.

Use for 100 lbs. of meat:

Sixty-one and three-quarter ounces salt, $2\frac{3}{4}$ oz. powdered saltpetre, 4 2-5 oz. white cane sugar. When treated in this manner the meat will become more of a gluish consistency, while the color will be heightened; it may be kept for a week without injuring its quality. When ready for sausagemaking the beef thus prepared is first finely chopped, then the pork added, chopped also, but less finely than the beef. The following is further added: $5\frac{1}{4}$ oz. white ground pepper, $2\frac{3}{4}$oz. finely ground coriander seed, three-fourths ounce mace; 5 pieces of garlic and 10 shallots rubbed up with salt, all to be mixed; also some finely chopped lemon peel is added to the sausage mass. Add as much water to the mixture as it willbear, then from 10 to 15 pounds of pounded meat, like that used for mortadelli. This should be beaten into a jelly with mallets. Knead up all together, from one side to the other for about one-half hour. This will brighten the color and render the mass very solid, notwithstanding the amount of water absorbed. In winter, the water to be worked in should be lukewarm. Fill into sheep casings not too narrow; should be stuffed full, and twisted off into sausages of about 3½ to 5 oz. each. Hang upon sticks and allow to dry several hours; in winter, in a warm room. The sausages should be very carefully smoked, as carelessness in this respect will make the skin hard. When the first smoke has gone off, and the shavings are just glowing, and the thick smoke shows a temperature of about 133° F., the sausages are quickly put in. They should be watched while smoking and not left in smoke longer than 20 or 25 minutes. At the end of that time the sausages should be of a chestnut-brown color. Immediately after smoking, the sausages are scalded in hot water for a few minutes, keeping them constantly in agitation, until they float on the water. Now they are hung upon clean sticks, and, for a few seconds only, are put into cold water. A hot sausage, if well made, on being bent should break open and let the juice escape freely. When served for the table they are made hot without being boiled, as the strong heat in smoking has already cooked them sufficiently.

VIENNA SAUSAGE (WIENERWURST)—ANOTHER RECIPE

Take 20 pounds veal, 70 pounds lean pork, 10 pounds fat pork and 1 pound potato flour; chop the whole fine and season the mass with 32 oz. salt and 12 oz. white pepper. Knead the mixture well as usual, adding from time to time small quantities of water. Stuff the mass into narrow casings and smoke 12 hours. Scald the sausages for 3 minutes and allow to cool in the usual way.

If garlic flavor is desired, the mass may be so seasoned.

For this sausage, trimmings from salt meats, etc., may also be used.

### LYONNAISE SAUSAGE

This sausage is very palatable, and when properly dried is as much liked as cervelat sausage. For 100 pounds use: 62¼ pounds pork, moderately lean; 25 pounds young beef, bruised in an iron dish, or on the block; 12½ pounds back-fat, cut into dice of about the size of a pea, and just slightly scalded. Add further: 3 pounds salt, 4½ oz. cane sugar and 2¼ oz. powdered saltpetre. Cut up and allow to stand for 48 hours in a cool place in summer, in a moderately warm one in winter.

Now chop the lean meat fine and spice as follows: 4½ oz. white pepper, 1 oz. white ginger, 1 oz.. mace, finely ground, 7 pieces leek with some salt, rubbed up together. Before adding the fat, the spice is thoroughly incorporated with a little water into the mass. Then add the back fat which has to be uniformly cut, mix it a little with the mass without rubbing, in order not to mash pieces of fat. Now stuff firmly into well-salted beef middle guts, 1½ feet long; wipe them dry carefully and smoke to a rich, red color; scald immediately and heat them up to 200° F. for half an hour.

When cold, this sausage will show wrinkles which are removed by just dipping the sausage in pairs for 15 seconds, into boiling hot water. Now again wipe dry and rub with a little cottonseed oil. If intended for shipment, the sausage should again be brought into cold smoke for 6 or 8 hours, which will make it keep better.

### FRANKFORTS

Use 70 pounds lean pork trmmings, 15 pounds lean beef trimmings, 5 pounds fat pork, 5 pounds veal. Chop well and add if necessary 2 pounds potato flour, to give the sausage sufficient moisture to prevent dryness.

Season with 25 oz. fine salt, 10 oz. ground white pepper, 2 oz. ground ginger, 2 oz. coriander seed.

Stuff in sheep casings or narrow hog casings. Smoke lightly and afterward merely heat up in boiling water in which has been dissolved a little bole or sausage dye, from 3 to 5 minutes is sufficient. Do not hang in too moist an atmosphere. The objection generally to such sausage is the extreme dryness when cooked, which is probably due to overcooking, in the majority of cases.

### FRANKFORT FRIED SAUSAGE

For every lot of 100 pounds use pork of young, light, firm hogs that contains much gelatine; use ham or shoulder meat, bellies and necks. Clean off the skin and bones the day before using and preserve the meat on hooks until wanted for use, in an airy room where it will cool and dry. Use about two parts lean meat and one part of fat meat. Chop to about half a walnut size, adding 49 2-5 oz. salt, 5¼ oz. pepper, 2 1-10 oz. mace. Continue chopping, wiping the knife frequently, and add 1 gallon of water while chopping; use more water if the mass remains too stiff. Reduce to about grain size, which is best observed by beating the mass flat with the palm of the hand, then break the mass apart a few times; this should be done without kneading it any more. Then put into stuffing machine and press down carefully, so as to remove any air in the mixture.

Fill into narrow hog casings previously well washed and freed from water; make casings full, not tieing them, but turning links off according to local custom, for instance, 4 or 5 pieces to the pound; that is, one pair weighing from 7 to 8 ounces. Leave a small butt end on each sausage, hang on clean sticks and allow to dry for 5 or 6 hours. Put in smoke of high temperature. The smoking house for these sausages should be quite large and roomy. At both sides of the shaft should be an air shaft with door about eight feet square, to smoke with a continuous draft of air. Use dry oak and beech shavings and have a temperature of about 72 to 77° F., until the sausage has assumed a reddish-yellow color, which will be obtained in from 8 to 10 hours.

If smoked too quickly, these sausages will not hold their color. Before using, they should be placed for 8 minutes in boiling water or until they feel firm to the touch. Fry in brown butter or butter fat for 6 minutes, allowing 3 minutes for each side, before turning them. If intended for immediate consumption, a little cardamom and finely-ground lemon peel may be added to the spicing.

### ROESTWURST

Take 11 pounds of raw, lean pork, 4½ pounds of good veal from the round, 3½ pounds of fat pork, and chop the mixture finely. Season with 6 oz. of salt and 2 oz. of ground pepper and mix well, adding a quart of cold water. Stuff in narrow hog or sheep casings. After tieing the ends together, they are divided in the middle and twisted there, thus forming a two-link sausage from the filled casing. They should then be smoked thoroughly for 2 to 4 hours. These sausages should not be kept longer than 8 days, as they become hard and dry. They are prepared for use by putting them in boiling water for 3 or 4 minutes.

### VIENNA KREEN SAUSAGE

Use for this 10 pounds firm veal, 10 pounds back fat and 20 pounds lean pork. Chop all together finely and spice with 2 1-10 oz. black pepper, three-quarter oz. saltpetre, one-third oz. mace, three-quarters oz. sugar and a few pieces of garlic and shallots. Mix up the mass with the desired amount of water and stuff into sheep casings. Twist off in pairs and then treat the same as Frankfort fried sausage.

A different flavor, required in some localities, is the addition of 8 oz. finely grated horseradish in place of the mace in the above seasonings.

### STRASSBURGER SAUSAGE.

With 30 pounds beef put 30 pounds veal and chop the mixture fine. To this add 20 pounds lean pork and chop with the beef and veal until moderately fine; 20 pounds of fat are now cut up into small pieces and mixed with the meats.

Season with 56½ oz. salt, 5½ oz. saltpetre, 7 oz. white pepper and 20 good-sized freshly crushed nutmegs. The whole is then chopped until the fat is cut into small dice. Water is mixed with the mass until it becomes moderately soft. Stuff into beef middles and allow the sausages to drain 3 or 4 hours before smoking. Or, they may be put into hot smoke at once and smoked to the required color, after which they are cooked for 15 or 20 minutes, removed from the kettle and hung up to cool. They are again scalded in boiling water for 10 or 15 seconds. This treatment will keep the casing smooth and tight.

### BOUDIN BLANC (WHITE SAUSAGE)

Equal parts of bellies, and lean, soft white pork are boiled together and finely chopped. For each 20 pounds of meat, 6 medium size onions are cut up and roasted in butter or butter fat until the pieces are clear or quite transparent. They should not have a yellow color. One-fourth pound wheat bread crusts are soaked until soft in 6 pints of cream and are added with the onions to the chopped meat. The yolks of 6 fresh eggs are also added to the mixture with the seasoning, which consists of 56 oz. salt, 4 oz. orange water, three-fourths ounce mace, one-third ounce ground cardamom seed and 1¾ oz. white pepper. The whole is thoroughly mixed, so that the mass is uniform throughout. Fill into narrow hog casings. Boil the sausages 15 minutes, wash them off with fresh water and place on the table to cool. These sausages should be kept in salt water until wanted for sale or shipment, as this preserves their white color.

When kept in this manner it is necessary to renew the brine every three days.

In seasoning this sausage the amount of salt may be varied to suit the requirements of the trade.

### CONEDENI

To 40 pounds finely chopped, salted, and well boiled pig skins are added 40 pounds veal and 20 pounds moderately fat pork. Chop the veal and pork separately before adding to the skin. Brine is now mixed with the mass and then water, until the whole mixture is moderately stiff, after being well kneaded. Pickle liquor may be used in place of brine and enough put in to produce the required salt flavoring of the sausage mass. Season with 9 oz. black pepper, $1\frac{1}{2}$ oz. coriander seed, $3\frac{1}{2}$ oz. caraway seed and three-fourths ounce mace. A few shallots may be used in the seasoning if so desired. Stuff into narrow hog casings, twist off in pairs and give these the same treatment as Frankfort sausages.

### MAINZER RED SAUSAGE

Neck or back fat, unskinned, is cut into narrow strips, 2 inches long and one-eighth inch in thickness. To make 100 pounds of stock, add to 70 pounds of above material 30 pounds skins from ham or back fat which have been boiled soft and finely chopped.

Warm the strips of fat, mix with the hog skin and season as follows: $65\frac{3}{4}$ oz. salt, $6\frac{2}{8}$ oz. white pepper, $6\frac{2}{8}$ oz. finely ground allspice, $3\frac{1}{2}$ oz. ground cloves, $2\frac{3}{4}$ oz. marjoram and $1\frac{1}{10}$ oz. ground mace.

Mix well with the mass, to which is added sufficient

hog blood to keep the mixture soft. More or less blood is mixed with this kind of sausage, according to the demands of the trade.

Fill the mass into hog stomachs or beef casings, and place immediately in boiling water. Cook until no blood appears when the sausage is pricked in the thickest part; when clear fat appears on pricking, the sausage is sufficiently cooked. It is not necessary to press this sausage when cooling.

If desired, pig tongues cut into strips may be added to the mass; sometimes pig snouts and ears are also used.

### THURINGIAN RED SAUSAGE

Twenty-eight pounds thick belly pieces moderately fat, are cooked half soft and then cut into dice about one-third of an inch square; 6 pounds boiled scraped pig skin fine together (if preferred some salted boiled tongue or salted boiled hearts, cut into similar dice, may be added); 16 pounds fresh blood are kept constantly stirred in a kettle until hot. Add the finely chopped skin, liver and lungs to the blood and mix all well. The belly meat should also be hot but free from broth when mixed into the mass. Now spice with $49\frac{1}{4}$ oz. fine salt, 5 oz. white pepper, $1\frac{3}{4}$ oz. finely ground marjoram, three-fourths ounce ground caraway seed, and $1\frac{3}{4}$ oz. best cloves. All the spices to be well mixed before incorporating with the mass. Fill quickly into wide hog casings or bungs, stuffing them loosely. Put the filled casings at once into boiling water, keeping them there constantly moving back and forth.

The sausages should be carefully pricked for air bubbles and boiled at 212° F. until on being pricked, clear fat exudes, showing the sausages to be thoroughly cooked. Allow them to cool and smoke cold, adding juniper berries to the smoking fire.

### HAMBURGER DRIED SMOKED BEEF

Use the meat near the tail, the rump steak; cut it up into suitable shape. Make pieces about 4½ inches wide by 16 inches long, of about 6 to 8 pounds weight, free from bones and fat. Rub this with salt and some white sugar, pack into a barrel, pour enough aromatic brine over it to cover all, weight it down, leaving about 1 inch of brine on top, then cover up tightly and allow to stand for 12 days. Whole rump steaks and pieces of that same size and weight, remain 3 weeks in the cure. When taken out the meat is allowed to lie some days without salting. It is still better to let it lie for 6 days, which will make it more tender. Wash off the meat, wipe dry with a cloth, hang in the air for 24 hours and then smoke with the same kind of smoke used for cervelat sausage. After a few days it will be ready for use. It shows a deep red color and is very tender.

### HAMBURGER KNACK SAUSAGE

For this sausage may be used cheek meat, hearts, sinewy and tough meat, and beef or calf lungs. For 100 pounds of stock use 53 oz. salt well mixed in, and 2¾ oz. saltpetre. After finely chopping add 14 oz. black pepper and 2 or 3 pounds potato flour with sufficient water to stiffen it. Mix and chop the mass thoroughly and fill into narrow beef casings. Make into small sausages weighing about a quarter of a pound each. Smoke in hot smoke, after which scald for 10 minutes.

### COBLENZER KNACK SAUSAGE

Use one-third or one-half pork, according to price. For 100 pounds use 50 pounds pork, moderately fat; 50 pounds beef from young animals. Each kind of meat is chopped up coarsely the day before, with the required quantity of salt and saltpetre, using 53 oz. of salt and 2¾ oz. of saltpetre. First chop the beef, then add the pork and spice as follows: 5¼ oz. white ground pepper; 1 2-5 oz. mace, finely ground; 1¾ oz. white ginger, finely ground; 1¾ oz. allspice, finely ground; 10 shallots; 10 pieces of garlic, rubbed up with salt. All are well mixed and incorporated with the mass.

Now chop until the fat appears in dice about the size of a pin-head; add as much water as it will bear, knead well until all is absorbed and the mass appears solid again; it is advisable to add 20 per cent. of pounded meat. Knead up well for half an hour; fill into narrow hog casings, not too tightly, and twist off about 5 or 6 sausages to a pound. Allow to dry in a good draft on sticks for several hours; in winter, in a heated room. Put into smoke of 100° F. Use oak and beech shavings. Smoke until of a bright yellow-red color, which will take about three-quarters of an hour. In smoking these sausages, it is advisable to use small smoking rooms. Cook, when desired, for 6 to 8 minutes in boiling water until they appear firm to the touch.

### SAUCISSES DE BOULOGNE.

Only the very best beef is used. It should be firm and of a dark red color. The beef is trimmed free from sinews and fat and 88 pounds chopped as finely as possible; 12 pounds clear salted bacon is cut into thick slices and added to this and both chopped together for some time. It is not advisable to chop the bacon separately and then mix it in by kneading. If this is done the fat bacon will not combine well with the meat and will, moreover, fall away from it when the sausage becomes dry. Season with 4 pounds salt, one-half pound coarsely ground pepper, 3¾ oz. saltpetre, 7¼ oz. sugar, 1¼ oz. ground ginger, 1¾ oz. ground cloves, 1½ oz. ground cardamom and seven-eighths ounce pulverized anise-seed. The spices are well kneaded into the mass.

Stuff the mixture into narrow or medium beef bung guts about 12 to 14 inches long, taking care to stuff the casings as tightly as possible. These sausages must be very carefully and slowly dried. It is advisable to hang them in a chill room or refrigerator for 5 or 6 days to allow them to set and shape themselves before drying.

Smoke them slowly in a cold smoke, afterwards hanging them in a place with a good draft for a few weeks. This latter treatment will make them firm and solid.

### PARISIAN SAUCISSE

For 100 pounds use 70 pounds moderately fat shoulder pork. Sprinkle 14 oz. salt over the meat and allow it to remain for some time in a temperature not over 60° F. Chop up moderately fine and add from time to time, while chopping, 15 quarts of water. In winter this water should be moderately warm. Knead the mass and then add more water, stirring it in quickly, not allowing the water to collect. If the latter remains unmixed with the sausage mass, when stuffed, the casings shrink and become tough. When most of the water is thoroughly incorporated, spice with $17\frac{3}{4}$ oz. salt, $12\frac{3}{16}$ oz. white pepper, $3\frac{1}{2}$ oz. pimento, 7 oz. sugar, and 4 teaspoonfuls each of ground cardamom, cloves, mace and coriander seed. In summer weather $1\frac{3}{4}$ oz. boracic acid are added with the spicing.

Add now the remainder of the water while constantly stirring. Allow the mass to rest in this condition for some time, about half an hour. Fill into medium-sized hog casings, stuffing loosely, twist off the sausages in pairs about 4 inches long and put them immediately into hot smoke for 10 to 15 minutes or until the sausages feel solid and break with a sharp crack. They are then scalded, and are ready for sale or shipment.

If it is desired, a small amount of basil and a few shallots may be added for those desiring such flavors.

### TONGUE SAUSAGE

For most sausages use fat and lean pork, which must be chopped into a paste and sprinkled with sufficient blood to moisten it well. To every 10 pounds of meat used must be added 20 pounds of tongues, cut into small pieces, somewhat larger than a good-sized pea. Fill into large sized casings and boil the sausages for about an hour. If pickled tongues are used they must be soaked in cold water for 16 hours before using.

### HAM, CHICKEN AND TONGUE SAUSAGE

Take 10 pounds of pork, 4 pounds of veal, 2 pounds of ox tongue, 4 pounds of fat, 2 pounds of ground rice, 2 pounds of scalded sausage meal, and 12 oz. of seasoning. Add to the above a quantity of chicken meat, salt, etc. Cut into small squares, mix in the scalded rice and put into the mixing machine, slowly adding the sausage meal and other ingredients. Chop very fine and fill the mixture into casings. Cook the sausages for 1 hour in water at a temperature of 200° F.

These casings may be colored before stuffing, or the casing of the filled sausage may be dyed as stated in the recipe for bologna sausage.

This sausage is also filled in weasands, lined with fat. The filled weasands are often dyed with bright attractive colors, as deep red, yellow, etc.

### GOTHAER TONGUE SAUSAGE

Sixty-six pounds of bacon are boiled sufficiently only to swell it. Cut it into thin strips and place these strips upon each other, allowing it to cool in this way. When cold cut it into small dice about the size of a pea, and place it in a strainer. Boiling hot water is now poured over it and the bacon allowed to drain free from excess of water. Thirty-three pounds soft boiled chopped pig skin with some fresh hog blood are then added to the bacon; the spicing is mixed and added to the chopped pig skin previous to mixing with the bacon, and consists of 6 3½ oz. salt. 6⅔ oz. white pepper, 3½ oz. allspice, 3½ oz. pulverized cloves, 2⅛ oz. finely powdered marjoram and 2⅛ oz. mace.

The ingredients must be well mixed. Fill the mass loosely into hog or small beef bladders and place in each bladder 2 or 3 salt, boiled pig tongues. Boil the sausages strongly, until upon pricking them, white, clear fat appears. When about half cooled, put them under pressure, which may be done by putting boards on top of them while on the bench and placing the required weights on top of these boards. Allow to cool under this pressure. Wipe dry and then put them in cold smoke.

Sometimes this is made with boiled cheek meat or raw bacon cut into small cubes, mixed with equal parts of boiled liver, skins or calf feet. Onions are added when this recipe is used in addition to the seasoning.

### APPETITE SAUSAGE

Take lean pork and trim it free from sinews. To each 8 pounds of pork add 1 pound of good bacon which has been chopped fine. With this chop 52¾ oz. walnut kernels which have been previously crushed or made fine. Season with 35¼ oz. salt, 5¼ oz. white pepper, 1¾ oz. cayenne pepper, three-fourths ounce white ginger and three-fourths ounce cloves. This seasoning is sufficient for each 100 pounds of stock. Moderately warm water is kneaded in until the whole mass is firm, when it is stuffed into narrow hog casings or wide sheep casings. The sausages are twisted off in pairs, so that each pair weighs about a quarter of a pound. They are allowed to hang for 1 or 2 hours, and then smoked in a cold smoke to a deep yellow color. When prepared for the table these sausages are scalded for 2 or 3 minutes.

This sausage should be made in limited quantities only,

as it does not remain in good condition for more than 3 days.

### SARDELLE SAUSAGE

Use pork and bacon, as in recipe for Appetite Sausage. The meat should be well cleaned from sinews and soft fat and chopped fine. For 100 pounds of mixture use as seasoning: 25 ⅝ oz. salt, three-fifths ounce white pepper, one-tenth ounce ground cloves, and one-tenth ounce mace. To this add 6¼ pounds sardelles, which need not be washed, but must be freed from bones and chopped fine. The whole is kneaded up together with a little water and well incorporated. These sausages are stuffed into narrow hog casings or wide sheep casings, and treated the same as those in previous recipe.

### LIVER CHEESE

This preparation requires a mould, made of tin or sheet iron, 12¾ inches long, 5½ inches high and 6 inches wide, provided with a well-fitting cover. This cover must be sufficiently close fitting to keep water from entering the mould when immersed in it.

The form is covered inside with a layer of raw white fat, cut thin. A cover of fat made to fit the mould is also provided. A form of the above dimensions will hold somewhat more than 10 pounds.

The mass for filling it is made as follows: 6 pounds raw hog liver is finely chopped; 4 pounds belly fat are added and chopped with the liver; 4 eggs are now mixed with the mass, which is spiced with 5 oz. salt, one-half ounce white pepper, 77 grains each of thyme and mace and 62 oz. ground cloves; 4 shallots, roasted yellow in butter fat, are rubbed up with fine salt, and this, with the rest of the seasoning, incorporated with the mass. The form is then filled to the brim with this and pressed down tightly, taking care, while so doing, to avoid the occurrence of air bubbles. The previously prepared cover of fat is now placed over it, and the metal cover, well greased inside, put on and tied up tightly in the mould.

It is then put into boiling water for 2½ hours, removed and allowed to stand without untieing or removing the cover for 10 or 12 hours, or until it is well set and chilled.

To remove the cheese from the mould dip it in hot water for half a minute, remove the cover and turn out carefully the moulded form on to a clean board or plate.

The liver cheese is ofen wrapped with tin foil to give it a more attractive appearance.

### COMMON HEAD CHEESE

Use soft-boiled pigskin or boiled calf feet. Coarsely chopped sinews may be also used if desired.

The material is cut into dice of moderate size or may be cut into small, thin strips. When mixing, add a small quantity of the strong broth obtained from the cooking of the materials.

Now prepare the following, which, for convenience, may be called Mixture No. 2: Mix in any desired proportion, salted hearts, cheek meat, ham trimmings, pickled meat trimmings, pig heads, snouts or ears, then skin and cut the cooked material into dice of about three-fourths of an inch.

Take for 100 pounds of stock 33 pounds of the first mixture and mix with 67 pounds Mixture No. 2. Thoroughly incorporate these and spice with 7 oz. white pepper, 7 oz. finely ground coriander seed and 10 or 15 chopped onions. Salt the mixture as required, allowing for the salt contained in the salted materials employed.

Stuff into prepared hog stomachs, boil strongly from 1 to 1¼ hours. When cooked, remove from kettle and wash free from any adhering fat. When somewhat cooled, press lightly in the usual manner under boards until cold.

### HEAD CHEESE—ANOTHER RECIPE

A very fine head cheese is made by using 90 pounds cheeks and 10 pounds skins, to be previously pickled for 3 or 4 days. Cut into strips and boil the meats three-quarters of an hour, the skins to be boiled 2 hours, and to be finely chopped. Spice with one-third of an ounce of juniper berries, 12 bay leaves, 7 oz. parsley, 7 oz. raw onions, the juice of 1 lemon, one-third ounce thyme, 4½ oz. allspice, 1¾ oz. cloves, 11 oz. pepper, and 1 pound salt.

The mixture is stuffed into previously cleaned and prepared hog stomachs, and treated as in former recipe.

### FINEST HEAD CHEESE

This is prepared as follows: 5 pounds each of beef and lean pork are chopped up with 3½ oz. salt and one-third of an ounce saltpetre, moderately fine and pressed in an earthenware jar. The mixture is allowed to remain for 2 days in a warm room. Two salted pigs' heads, a few salted pigs' feet and 15 pounds pig tongues are soaked for a short time and cooked. The bones are removed from the heads and feet and the white skin from the tongues. Cut all into medium sized dice, or the tongues may be cut into long thin strips. Six pounds chopped, boiled pig skins are now added to the above and mixed well.

For every pound of mass add three-fourths ounce white pepper, 15 grains mace and the quantity of salt required for the material. The juice of a lemon and a few finely cut laurel leaves may also be added if desired.

Knead well and fill into beef bung guts rather tightly. Cook for 1½ to 2 hours and then press until cold. Wipe the head cheese and smoke lightly.

### FRANKFORT TONGUE PRESS CHEESE

Hams or shoulders freed from bones are chopped up fine with salt, saltpetre and sugar.

For each 100 pounds of meat use 61¾ oz. salt, 2½ oz.

best saltpetre, 5 oz. cane sugar. Add 10 pieces of leek, and after chopping the mixture together coarsely, allow it to remain for 24 hours in a closed receptacle, pressing the mass firmly together. After this time has elapsed the meat assumes a rich red color. Now chop very fine, and while chopping add the spicing in the following proportions: 6¼ oz. white ground pepper, 1¾ oz. ground mace, 1½ oz. ground ginger and 1 oz. of pulverized cardamom.

Then cut about 5 tongues having a red color, into large dice, and with 10 handfuls well peeled pistachio nuts, add carefully to avoid bruising the tongue pieces. Then fill the mass into beef casings 10 inches long and carefully close them. They are parboiled for 1½ to 1¾ hours, until after pricking, the exuding juice is clear and white.

When cool, smoke as desired. A few handfuls of juniper berries added to the fire while smoking improves the flavor of the cheese.

This preparation has an attractive appearance and is very palatable.

### BRUSSELS MOSAIC SAUSAGE

Great care should be exercised in the preparation of this sausage, which, besides being a much liked delicacy, is an ornament for every show window, when properly cut. Use ham or shoulder meat, free from sinews, chop up coarsely with salt, saltpetre and cane sugar, and add one-fourth lean veal. For 100 pounds of meat of good, firm quality from light hogs use 3½ pounds of salt, 2½ oz. best saltpetre and 5¼ oz. cane sugar. The coarsely hashed meat is set aside for 24 to 30 hours, having been firmly pressed together in a stone vessel to give it a nice red color. Then chop up to about grain size and while chopping add the following spice, which should be previously mixed: 5½ oz. white pepper, 1¾ oz. mace, 1 2-5 oz. ginger and seven-eighths of an ounce of cardamom. Mix well and fill into long-shaped hog or beef bladders about 6 inches in diameter and about 7 inches long. Stuff three-fourths full; the opening should be large enough to easily introduce the following additions. These are about 5 inches long and consist of nice, red, boiled ox-tongue, of which the thicker part is cut up into long square shapes and coated with fine raw fat. Also introduce some thin, fine blood-orange Frankfurters, thin, fine Liver Sausage and Mett Sausage. See that all are inserted parallel to each other. This is facilitated by first boring a hole into the mass with a wet stick somewhat thicker than the additions referred to. Otherwise the fat will separate from the material. String up carefully, smoke in light smoke for 1 hour at about 63° F., and then boil up in a kettle for 1¾ hours. Keep the sausage in a straight position, so as to keep the added substances in their right place; to make it more durable, give the finished sausage a light smoking, using juniper berries with the smoke.

### PRESSED SAUSAGE

Use moderately fat pork, cut up about the size of a pea; shoulders or trimmings may be used; allow to remain several days mixed with the usual proportion of salt, saltpetre and sugar, as noted under Brussels Mosaic Sausage.

Take 20 pounds of the above, add to it 40 pounds of a mixture of boiled, salted snouts, ears and cheek fat, and also 12 pounds boiled, salted pig tongues. All the material is to be cut up in dice about half the size of a walnut. To the above mixture is then added 20 pounds soft-boiled pig skin, chopped moderately fine. If desired the skin may be replaced by chopped calf feet.

The whole is now kneaded thoroughly, adding to it, from time to time, 2 gallons very strong broth. Spice as follows: 7 oz. white ground pepper, 2 1-10 oz. mace, 2¾ oz. powdered coriander seed, 11¼ oz. shallots, rubbed up with salt and a little finely chopped lemon peel.

As most of the material is salt meats, due allowance must be made for this in seasoning the mass with salt. It is not possible to give here the exact amount to be added. This must be regulated by the manufacturer, who can judge best of the saltness of his working material.

The mixture is thoroughly kneaded to a uniform mass, which is filled loosely into cleaned and prepared hog stomachs, bladders or beef guts. The filled stomachs and bladders are cooked in water at 208° F. for 1½ to 1¾ hours, according to their size; and the filled beef casings at the same temperature for 1 to 1¼ hours. Any air bubbles in the sausages should be removed by careful pricking.

After boiling, and when cooling, turn the sausages from time to time to prevent the liquid inside them from settling in any one part. Frequent turning keeps the broth well mixed throughout the sausage.

The sausages are weighted in the usual manner while cooling.

If intended for immediate consumption or for local use, this sausage may be kept for a limited time without smoking, but if the sausages are to be shipped or stored, they should be put into cold smoke for a short time.

### VEAL SAUSAGE

To 10 pounds young dark-colored veal add 5 pounds bacon, and cut up the mixture moderately fine. When in this condition add 2 or 3 stale baker's rolls prepared in the usual manner for filling, and chop the whole mixture fine. Add of spice: 1¾ oz. white pepper, three-quarters of an ounce nutmeg, and 6⅛ oz. salt. Mix well and stuff into narrow hog casings.

In some cases the ground nutmeg is replaced by lemon, 1 oz. being chopped very fine and added to the mixture; or a few drops of oil of lemon may be added in place of fresh lemon.

### SALAMI—GENUINE ITALIAN RECIPE

Forty pounds of belly pieces without the soft fat are coarsely chopped with 20 pounds back fat, only a small quantity of salt being added and 2 1/10 oz. saltpetre, until the back fat is about the size of a bean. Add now 30 pounds freshly chopped beef and pack the mass on a table; or, balls of about 10 pounds may be made of the mass and tied up in clean muslin and hung in an airy, well-ventilated room for 24 hours. Then work the mass over again, adding to it 8½ oz. good red wine (strained free from sediment, if any), a few pieces of finely rubbed garlic, a few shallots, 2 oz. fresh, finely chopped basil, 7 oz. ground white pepper, 1⅔ oz. ground cloves and 1¾ oz. sugar. Wide beef casings are soaked for a day, previous to filling, in white or cider vinegar; when ready for use they are well rinsed and stuffed like cervelat sausage, taking care to press the mass as tightly as possible in the casings. A few hours after filling, wind a string around the sausages and put in brine for 10 to 16 hours, dependent upon the size. They are then removed and hung in a cool, dry, well-ventilated room, which is kept at an even temperature. After hanging 14 days they are taken down, washed, and each sausage separately dipped into lukewarm mutton tallow. They are again hung up. In this condition these sausages will keep for years.

It is essential during the course of manufacture to keep the temperature as even as possible.

### SALAMI—HUNGARIAN

For each 100 pounds use 75 pounds of dark lean pork freed from sinews. This is salted with 2 pounds salt and 2⅜ oz. saltpetre for 2 days. It is then well pressed to free it from excess of moisture, after which it is chopped into pieces about the size of a pea; 25 pounds thinly sliced bacon is added, chopped up a little with the meat, and the mixture spiced as follows: One and three-quarter pounds salt, ½ pound sugar, 5¼ oz. ground pepper, three-quarter ounce paprika, three-quarter ounce boracic acid (or 1¾ oz. borax). The mixture is thoroughly chopped until the bacon fat is very finely divided, the mass being frequently turned. It is immediately put into narrow beef casings or bung guts. The casings should be filled tightly, avoiding air bubbles, and carefully tied. The finished sausage is then rubbed with salt and put in pickle for 10 days, in a temperature of 54° F. Then removed and hung up to dry out for 14 days in a temperature of 60° F. It is finally smoked for 10 days in cold smoke and again hung in a temperature of 60° F. After two or three weeks these sausages are not further affected by heat.

Hungarian Salami is generally made in the cool season, between October and April.

### SALAMI DI VERONA

Use as follows for each 100 pounds: Thirty-six pounds of lean beef freed from sinews, 36 pounds of lean pork also freed from sinews, 28 pounds of back fat, sliced to about one-half inch pieces.

For spicing use 63½ oz. of salt, 5¾ oz. of white pepper, 5 oz. of powdered cane sugar, 2⅛ oz. of powdered potassium saltpetre and 4 oz. of old French cognac.

This spicing is carefully blended before adding it to the mass.

First chop the beef; then all the meat and fat to about half walnut size; now add the salt and spice mixture and continue chopping and turning the mass until it is chopped to about pea size. The knife should be frequently wiped off in order to remove particles of adhering meat which would cause inequality in the finished sausages. Before chopping, the block should be well rubbed with five or six pieces of good garlic, or until the block is well permeated with this flavor.

Use beef middles, which are tied after stuffing (with double thread twine), from thick to thin ends. Now treat the same as cervelat sausages, but do not smoke, drying the sausage instead, from 4 to 5 weeks.

### MUNICH CERVELAT

Take 50 pounds of veal and chop up very fine. To this is added 50 pounds pork which need not be chopped so fine as the veal. Spice the mixture with $2\frac{3}{10}$ oz. saltpetre, $11\frac{3}{4}$ oz. white pepper and the necessary amount of salt. Mix 16 pounds fat, cut into dice, with the mass and thoroughly incorporate. Fill loosely into beef middle guts, and make small sausages nearly round in shape, forming a chain. Smoke over a hot fire and then scald.

### METT SAUSAGE

This is generally made in the cool season from October to April. For 100 pounds use 60 pounds of beef and 40 pounds of pork.

Use the trimmings or residue from the manufacture of cervelat or salami sausages, cleaning the beef, however, from any tallow. The pork may be used fat. First chop the beef for 1 hour, mixing with it 70 ounces of salt; next add the pork, chop up all together and season with 14 oz. salt, $12\frac{1}{4}$ oz. pepper, 70 oz. sugar, $5\frac{3}{8}$ oz. saltpetre, $5\frac{3}{8}$ oz. borax (or $3\frac{3}{4}$ oz. boracic acid may be used in place of the borax). Continue chopping for 1 hour, cleaning the knife frequently and kneading in these portions with the rest of the mass. Allow the mixture to remain 2 hours before stuffing, in a temperature of about 60° F. After the requisite time has elapsed fill into bung guts. Hang up for a week to dry out, then smoke with cool smoke for 5 days.

### BEST METT SAUSAGE

A distinction is made between Brunswick or Thuringian Mett Sausage and the Dutch sausage. The former is finer. For both kinds the residues left from making cervelat sausage are used, which material, owing to its sinewy and fatty nature is not well adapted for some kinds of sausage. The following recipe is for the latter class of sausage:

To each 100 pounds half fat pork use 63½ oz. salt, 5⅜ oz. white ground pepper, 4 oz. cane sugar, 2 oz. powdered saltpetre. Mix all this before chopping, then chop the meat to about half a walnut size, add the spice and continue chopping until about pea size, frequently turning the mass upside down on the block. Stuff tightly into narrow hog casings, to weigh about 1 pound to 1½ pounds, and tie the ends together; dry for about a week and then smoke in cold light smoke until reddish yellow.

### BRUNSWICK METT SAUSAGE

For Brunswick Mett Sausage, use less sinewy meat; select about two-thirds lean, one-third fat pork from the hind or fore leg, or from sides. Use the same quantities as above, *i. e.*, for 100 pounds of meat, 63½ oz. salt, 5⅜ oz. white pepper, finely ground; 4 oz. cane sugar, 2 oz. ground saltpetre. Mix and add same when the mass is chopped, to about pea size, and chop up latter as fine as the material in cervelat sausage. Treat altogether like cervelat sausage, but fill into narrow hog casings of large size, to weigh about 1½ to 2 pounds each. Dry and smoke the same as cervelat sausage. The casings may be fresh, or well salted, but should not be too narrow.

### BRUNSWICK METT SAUSAGE—ANOTHER RECIPE

This sausage may be made at all seasons. Pork only is used, half of which is shoulder meat, the rest ham or similar trimmings. For 100 pounds mixture, spice with

1 pound of salt, 12½ oz. white pepper, one-half ounce boracic acid, 10½ oz. sugar, 3½ oz. saltpetre, 4 teaspoonfuls each of ground cardamom, mace and cloves. Chop the mass for 1½ hours. Do not knead any more after this and do not wipe the knife—two important points to remember.

Fill the mixture into clean, narrow beef casings to form the necessary rings. Allow the sausages to dry in a good draft of air, or in the sun; too much heat from the latter is, however, to be avoided. Put in cold smoke for 5 or 6 days.

### SUMMER SAUSAGE

To four parts of good beef and four parts lean pork add two parts of the amount of fat pork or bacon. Trim the beef free from sinews and fat; chop fine; then add the lean pork; chop again and add the fat pork in small squares or dice. Chop until well mixed, adding salt and pepper to suit individual trade. Whole peppers are added in seasoning this mass, in addition to the ground spice, but total amount of seasoning should not exceed 2 pounds for every 100 pounds of meat. Stuff into hog bungs or beef middle casings very tightly and hang in the open air for 4 or 5 days. Smoke very slowly 3 to 5 days at a moderate heat. To remove the white appearance that these sausages sometimes have after being kept some time, rub the casings with a cloth saturated with fat or cottonseed oil. This sausage may be kept, if hung up, from 4 to 6 weeks in winter time without being smoked. By making summer sausage the same as above, but allowing the meat to be very coarse, the product may be called salami. That will remain in good condition perhaps a greater length of time. Care should be taken not to allow any unfilled places in the sausage casing and no water should be added to the mass. Casings to be used for summer sausages should be thoroughly soaked in water 24 hours before using, to entirely remove the salt in which they may have been packed.

For some trade and localities this sausage is flavored with garlic.

### BEST BLOCK SAUSAGE

For each 100 pounds stock use 60 pounds pork, moderately fat, from fore or hind leg or belly; 40 pounds lean bull beef free from sinews. First chop the beef fine, add the pork, chopped to half walnut size, and then season as follows: 70½ oz. salt, 5⅜ oz. white pepper, 4 oz. powdered cane sugar, 2¼ oz. powdered saltpetre, 4 pieces best garlic finely ground, 1 ¾ oz. cardamom, 8 tablespoonfuls rum. Mix well in a dish, add to the mass and chop up (constantly turning the mass), to about bean size. The knife should always be wiped, as with cervelat sausage, in order to insure a homogeneous appearance of the mass. The mass should not be kneaded, but only broken open. Now stuff firmly, using good salted beef middle guts about 13 inches long; allow the sausages to hang several hours, then put into good brine for 6 hours, or they may be rubbed instead with fine salt; put side by side upon a board and set aside for 12 hours in the cooler. Then wash roughly with cold water and wipe dry with cloth. Now allow to dry in an airy place about 50 to 55° F. until the mass shows red through the transparent casing; now smoke in cold smoke with beech and oak shavings, mixed with a few juniper berries. This sausage should be smoked lightly to a light yellow red. All the meat used should be from firm, heavy, well-grown animals, the same as with cervelat sausage. The casings should also be treated the same as they are for cervelat sausage.

### LIVER SAUSAGE

Take half a dozen pigs' heads, 50 pounds cheek meat,

25 pounds trimmings, and cook well until the head meat separates easily from the bone; add to this 25 pounds liver, well scalded, and chop up all together, until very fine. For each 100 pounds of this mixture use 2 pounds salt, one-half pound pepper, one-fourth pound cloves, and a small quantity of marjoram. Mix well, stuff in bung guts and cook for half an hour.

Onions may be added to the above mass if such flavor is desired.

### BRUNSWICK SARDINE LIVER SAUSAGE

For 100 pounds use 32 pounds hog liver, 28 pounds lean pork, 16 pounds raw leaf lard, 24 pounds fresh pork fat and 2 pounds good sardines which have been well washed and prepared, free from bones.

Cut the liver into narrow strips and wash it with cold water; then scald it thoroughly and again scald to extract any blood remaining in it. This point is essential in order that a fine white sausage may be obtained. Allow the liver to drain and then chop fine. The lean pork should be partially cooked before using, taking care not to boil it too soft. This is chopped moderately fine and added to the liver. The raw leaf lard, also previously scalded, is now added, and finally the boiled pork fat. The whole is now chopped up very fine and the seasoning and prepared sardines added and thoroughly mixed with the mass.

The seasoning consists of 5 oz. salt, $5\frac{1}{2}$ oz. ground white pepper, $2\frac{1}{10}$ oz. ground white ginger, $1\frac{2}{8}$ oz. ground mace, $2\frac{1}{10}$ oz. finely ground marjoram and $1\frac{2}{8}$ oz. thyme, finely ground.

Fill into short middleguts of about 10 inches in length, not too tightly, and cook from 25 to 30 minutes in boiling water.

These sausages should not be pricked. After cooking they are immediately put into cold water which has to be frequently changed until the sausages are thoroughly cooled and are firm.

### FRANKFORT LIVER SAUSAGE—HAUSMACHER

All material excepting the finely cut fat is used in the raw condition.

Ten pounds raw hog liver freed from veins, 2 onions finely scraped, and 7 pounds raw neck or cheek meat are used. It is preferable to use the fatty part of the latter meats. The liver is first chopped and the raw fat then added and the chopping continued. Then 3 pounds fat cut into small dice are added to the mixture.

The seasoning is previously mixed before incorporating with the mass, and consists of 10 oz. fine salt, 10 oz. fine white pepper, 170 grains thyme and 135 grains best cloves. The whole is then chopped up well. Stuff loosely into beef middles about 13 inches long. The sausages are then put in water kept near the boiling point, for 40 to 45 minutes.

To ascertain if they are sufficiently cooked, prick with a needle or awl, when the juice will be perfectly clear if the sausage has received the required amount of cooking.

This sausage is never exactly white, but it should have a light, grayish appearance. When smoked it is considered a great delicacy. In making and finishing, it has to be carefully treated or it is liable to become sour.

### FINE FRANKFORT LIVER SAUSAGE

Use 7 pounds raw hog liver free from blood, 5 pounds boiled veal from the breast, neck and cheeks, which should not be boiled too soft; also calf lights. Calf sweetbreads may be used, but ordinarily they are too expensive. Chop the liver first very fine, add 12 to 15 roasted shallots or 2 roasted onions, add to meat, mix, and add further 4 pounds boiled hog gut fat or fat hog cheeks.

When all is finely chopped and mixed add 4 pounds boiled fresh fat cut into small dice. To these 20 pounds add 10 oz. salt, 1 oz. fine white pepper, 170 grains of fine white ginger, 200 grains marjoram finely bruised, 136 grains mace bruised, 170 grains thyme finely rubbed.

Mix the spices first, add to the mass, mix well, and fill into wide, white hog casings, or hog bungs, but not too tight. Boil for a half to three-quarters of an hour, according to size of sausage, until the juice shows perfectly clear on pricking. Do not prick too much, as it will waste the juice. After boiling put at once into cold water, which has to be renewed, until the sausage is perfectly cooled, feels firm and appears uniformly white.

### COMMON FRANKFORT LIVER SAUSAGE

A good recipe for common Frankfort liver sausage is as follows: Remove the skin and hard veins from beef liver, hog liver freed from gall veins, and from hog or beef lungs cut off the hardest part of the trachea (wind-pipe) and pare off the inner bloody part. Take equal parts, chop fine, add 6 to 8 onions, trimmings of various kinds, scraps, and mix all by chopping. For each 40 pounds liver stuffing, use 12 pounds liver, 12 pounds raw lungs, 10 pounds fat scraps and 6 pounds fat cut into dice. Spice with 21 oz. salt, 2½ oz. pepper, three-quarter ounce marjoram, four-fifths ounce thyme. First mix the spices well, add to the mass and then chop. In winter a few spoonfuls of fat-broth are preferably added. Put the mass in beef or hog casings and boil the sausage until, on being pricked, the juice appears clear. Then clean off with fresh water. For a large quantity of liver sausage use beef lungs, calf heads, etc., which have been boiled the day before.

### LIVER SAUSAGE WITH ONIONS

This sausage is prepared as follows: For 100 pounds use 28 pounds liver cut into slices, well washed and scalded lightly in hot water; 20 pounds cooked soft fat (preferably gut fat), 12 pounds bacon, slightly boiled, cut into fine dice, and 40 pounds lean meat. For this latter meat use one part soft boiled beef lungs, one part well-scalded calf lungs or hearts, one part boiled meat or calf heads, calf neck or breast, the latter not too soft. First chop the liver fine, then chop 10 or 12 onions, boil the gut fat, cut into pieces about bean size; now roast the onions slowly in the gut fat in an enameled dish until the onions are light yellow, keeping the mass constantly stirred. Add the roasted portion to the whole mass and chop up fine. Spice with 53 oz. fine salt, 5⅜ oz. white ground pepper, 2¾ oz. finest ground marjoram, and 1 oz. mace ground fine. Mix and knead into the mass. The bacon is scalded; more may be taken if desired. This mass, when finished, will be perfectly white. Fill into beef middle guts or bung guts or into hog casings of desired width and length. Cook the sausages at 210° F. for 25 or 30 minutes. Leave in cold water after boiling, until perfectly cool, renewing the water constantly. The lungs, hearts, kidneys, etc. used for this sausage should be well soaked the day before and scrupulously cleaned.

### GOTHAER LIVER SAUSAGE

For 100 pounds stock use 70 pounds moderately fat fresh pork and 30 pounds hog liver. Chop the raw liver for 1 hour, or until air bubbles form in it. Now add the pork and 1 pound onions, and chop until it is not possible to make the mass finer. It should be very smooth and spread as easily as lard.

Season with 1 pound salt, 14 oz. white pepper, 1¼ oz. each of mace and cloves and one-quarter ounce rubbed thyme. Mix well and stuff loosely in middles. This should be done quickly to avoid the action of the salt on the mass. The sausages are cooked in water kept at 200°

F. for 1¼ hours. They are then removed, cooled in the usual manner in cold water and dried in the open air. Or if desired, they may be smoked for 1 or 2 days.

In making the mass for this sausage salt should never be added to the meats while chopping. The moisture in them dissolves the salt and forms a brine which acts on the mass and gives to it a very undesirable reddish color.

### BRUNSWICK LIVER SAUSAGE

For 100 pounds stock use 34 pounds hog liver and 66 pounds pork bellies or neck. Cut the liver into small strips and scald in hot water 200° F. Allow it to drain and then chop for three-quarters of an hour. Skin the boiled pork, freed from water, and chop it with the liver for another three-quarters of an hour.

Boil 52 oz. onions with 6 pounds lard and add the resultant liquid, strained, to the mass, and season with 1 pound salt, 14 oz. white pepper, one-quarter ounce rubbed thyme, one-half ounce rubbed marjoram, one-quarter ounce each of cardamom, coriander seed, cloves and mace.

Stuff the mass loosely into middles or bungs. The sausages are allowed to cook in water at 200° F. for 1 hour, taking care not to let the water rise above this temperature. After this time has elapsed remove the sausages and place them in cold water until hard.

This sausage may be dried, or, if desired, may be smoked.

### STRASSBERG TRUFFLE AND GOOSE LIVER SAUSAGE

This sausage should be made in small quantities from time to time, in order to keep it juicy. Make in batches of about 10 pounds. Use 2 pounds light calf liver cut into thin slices, boiled a little in hot water, chop up somewhat; then add 8 pounds pork from the belly and neck half fat, half lean, of young, solid hogs; chop the pork very fine.

Then roast to a light yellow in fresh butter 4 pieces shallots, rub them fine with a pinch of salt, and add same to the mass.

Then take 5¼ oz. salt, one-half ounce finely ground white pepper, 76 grains best white ginger, 76 grains mace, finely ground.

Mix well with the mass; this sausage, which is regarded as a fashionable delicacy, should not be too sharp in taste.

Then cut 7 oz. nice, red, salted boiled tongues into fine dice, about half-grain size, add 1¾ oz. Perigord truffle in dice about the same size and mix it to the mass.

When all is well distributed, throw firmly into the stuffing machine and stuff lightly into very wide fresh hog guts. The sausage when finished should not be longer than 1 foot; if it is made longer, there is danger of its being dry and parboiled at the thin ends.

Boil the sausage from three-quarters of an hour to an hour, according to thickness; on being pricked, the fat which exudes should be perfectly clear and white. Boil in clean broth; never boil these sausages with blood sausage. When finished, put into cold water, which should be frequently changed until the sausage is perfectly cold. This procedure keeps the juice nice and white.

### GOOSE LIVER SAUSAGE

For 10 pounds use 5 pounds goose livers cut into dice or small squares about the size of a walnut. Use the same mass as given in the recipe for Strassberg Truffle and Goose Liver Sausage, but do not mix the layer with it. On a flat layer of mass, put a layer of cut goose liver close together, then again a layer of mass; then liver once more, and so on until all the livers are incorporated into the mass; make into balls and fill carefully into the stuffing machine, being careful to avoid mashing the tender livers, and fill into very wide hog guts.

Goose liver sausage and truffle liver sausage are always made at the same time, using the same mass for both and taking as much of the mass for goose liver sausage as will suffice for livers on hand. Boil and treat like truffle sausage. In cutting goose livers it should be noticed that the livers can only be cut smoothly when the knife is put into hot water before every cut. Before boiling the sausages, prick with a fork or fine awl for the whole length, to allow the air to escape when boiling the sausage.

### FINEST STRASSBERGER GOOSE LIVER PIE

The following is a most excellent recipe: One-quarter, half and whole sized bowls are used for these pies. They are covered inside with a thin layer of fat; then a piece of fresh fat is cut so as to fit on top as a cover. For 10 pounds use 5 pounds lean meat from hams (free from sinew) of firm, young hogs, then 5 pounds from the belly. Chop very fine; add 3 shallots, roasted light yellow in fresh butter, and rubbed fine with a pinch of salt, 6¼ oz. fine salt, one-half ounce finely ground white pepper, 61 grains fine white ginger, 46 grains mace, 77 grains powdered dried mushrooms.

Mix the spice and incorporate well into the mass. Now begin filling the bowls by first introducing a layer about one-third of an inch thick. On this put nice white goose liver three-quarters of an inch thick, intermixed with Perigord Truffle.

Cover with a layer of mass and on this again put liver and truffle, and so on until the bowl is filled. The filling should be stuffed firmly but cautiously, so as not to mash the livers. The truffles are cut to about one-half walnut size. When the bowl is filled, close with the cover of fat, previously prepared; on this press the cover of the bowl and fasten around the opening with moist dough.

For whole bowls the same proceeding is followed, but the liver is cut twice as thick.

The bowls are now cooked in an open vessel; the water being kept within an inch of the cover, until after about 1½ hours, a pricking needle, inserted at the opening, when withdrawn, remains clean. While cooling, the cover is weighted down to make it tight. The bowls are to be carefully cleaned and the dough removed from the opening, in place of which melted lard is now put into the opening of the cover, so as to close all cavities. The cover is then fastened with warm lard.

### SCHWERINER LIVER SAUSAGE

Use equal parts of bellies, fat and lean. Also kidneys, tongues, and all cooked soft. The liver is chopped raw and rubbed through a sieve. The meat and fat is cut into small dice and the kidneys finely chopped. Spice to the desired taste with fine salt, pepper, cloves, and a small quantity of finely rubbed thyme and marjoram. To this add the fat skimmed off the broth in which the meats were cooked. The mass is filled loosely into casings, the sausages boiled for half an hour and then cooled in the usual manner in cold water.

The sausage may be smoked if desired.

### SCHWERINER LIVER SAUSAGE—ANOTHER RECIPE

A hog liver is well cooked and chopped up fine. To this add three times its weight of lean meat. Neck, belly or shoulder meat may be used. Add the same weight of bacon, cut in dice, as the liver. Now add the same quantity of lard in which several onions have been roasted. Spice as usual, with salt, white pepper, allspice and a small quantity of ground cardamom seed and marjoram. Fill into narrow beef casings and treat as in the previous recipe.

## FRANKFORT SAUSAGE

To make 100 pounds of Frankfort sausage take 75 pounds of pork and 25 pounds of beef. Cheek, neck or any other kind of beef may be taken without endangering the quality of the sausage. To the mass add 1½ pounds of salt, one-quarter pound of cloves and one-quarter pound of mace, and all the water the meat may require. By using from 2 to 5 pounds of potato flour the quantity of water added may be largely increased. Mix well and fill into sheep casings. Hang the sausages in an airy place for about half an hour to dry, then smoke for about half an hour over a light fire, and, finally, smoke an additional half hour over hot fire. To prepare for use place in boiling water, allowing them to remain therein for about 5 minutes. These sausages should not be kept too long, as they become dry and unpalatable in a comparatively short time.

## FRANKFORTER BLOOD STOMACH

Use bacon only half cooked, cut in pieces of size of about half of a pea, soak in hot water, so as to remove all fat, and let drain until the bacon is perfectly dry. Add one-third soft boiled finely chopped pig skin, mix with the bacon and spice as follows for 100 pounds: Sixty-two ounces salt, 7 oz. pepper, 3½ oz. fine cloves, 3½ oz. fine peppermint, 2½ oz. fine marjoram, 2½ oz. finely ground mace, 30 pieces of leek finely bruised.

Mix the spice, add to the mass, mix and add the necessary amount of hog blood (about one-fifth of the whole quantity); knead the mass well. Fill into hog stomachs, bladders or beef guts, three-quarters full. The water should be boiling and the sausage being filled and tied, is brought into the kettle and slightly stirred; boil until on pricking no blood, but perfectly clear fat, is obtained; remove the sausages and wash them. Turn the product freely to hasten the cooling.

Always use fresh blood. The best is hog blood; calf, mutton or beef blood can also be used, but not the blood from "kosher" cattle. This blood frequently contains liquid excrements. The kettle in which these are boiled should not be used for any other kind of sausage.

If the blood is not used up at once foam begins to form on the surface, which should be skimmed off. The blood should frequently be poured from one vessel to another with the addition of some salt, which deepens the color; it should be strained before using.

This kind of sausage is frequently handsomely embellished, and is quite an adornment for the market.

### FRANKFORT YELLOW SAUSAGE

For 100 pounds use 70 pounds hog bellies and 30 pounds brains. The bellies should be from young, firm hogs, not too fat; chop fine. Add either hog, veal or beef brains, previously freed from the bloody skin. Chop up all together very fine and add the spice while chopping. Use 3 pounds salt, $6\frac{1}{4}$ oz. freshly ground, fine, white pepper, $1\frac{3}{4}$ oz. mace, finely ground. Knead the mass thoroughly, fill into nice, white, fresh hog guts $1\frac{1}{2}$ feet long; get it airtight, but leave enough margin for the casing to yield when the inner mass presses on it in cooking. Then boil in hot water for 45 to 60 minutes, according to thickness. Try by pricking whether the juice is clear, but avoid useless pricking.

This sausage has to be carefully sliced when cold. It is an ornament for every shop window.

### GARLIC SAUSAGE

For 100 pounds stock use 40 pounds beef trimmings, which should be chopped while still warm from the slaughtered bullock after the manner previously described under meats (Chapter III.). To the chopped meat add 20 pounds lean pork trimmings and again chop. Knead the mass well and add from time to time 30 pounds water. In winter this should be warm, but in summer cold water may be used. An extra quality of meat trimming may take up still more water.

The consistency of the mass should now be tested. If the meat breaks when allowed to drop, too much water has been added. The mass when dropped should form a long, elastic band.

The addition of potato flour will bring it, when too moist, back to the proper condition. To the mixture add the usual quantity of salt, pepper and allspice as seasoning, with the further addition of $5\frac{1}{2}$ oz. saltpetre and the desired quantity of finely rubbed garlic.

Mix well and fill firmly into narrow beef casings, forming rings. Hang up to dry a few hours in summer, and in cold weather for 10 or 12 hours. Smoke with a low, smouldering fire until the sausages are somewhat dried out, then increase the heat in the smoke-house until the sausages become firm. Remove and put in water of 200° F. for 10 minutes. Cool by placing them in cold water.

### BEST GARLIC SAUSAGE

Forty pounds veal are chopped up 12 hours before wanted for use in making the sausage, adding to the veal 14 oz. salt and $5\frac{1}{2}$ oz. saltpetre and the mixture packed in a trough or barrel.

To the above, when ready for use, add 30 pounds fat pork and chop the mixture well; 30 pounds of water are then added in the same manner as described in previous recipe. Spice the mass as follows: $12\frac{3}{10}$ oz. white pepper, $3\frac{3}{4}$ oz. boracic acid, $17\frac{3}{4}$ oz. sugar and one-half ounce each of ground cardamom, mace and cloves. Rub up 2 pieces of peeled garlic with 7 oz. salt; add to the spiced mixture and thoroughly mix.

Fill into narrow hog casings and twist off in pairs. The sausages are first lightly smoked for 1 hour; the heat is then gradually raised until after smoking 3 hours they become firm.

They are cooked in boiling water for 15 minutes, removed and allowed to remain in cold water until thoroughly cool.

### SILESIAN OR BRESLAU KNACK SAUSAGE

The mixture for this is the same as that for garlic sausage, adding to the mass, however, 10 pounds finely chopped bacon. The sausages are filled loosely and twisted off in pairs about 4 inches in length. They are dried and further treated the same as garlic sausage.

### HORSERADISH SAUSAGE

Use the same mass as for garlic sausage, but in place of the garlic use horseradish. To every 100 pounds of sausage mass add 4 pounds finely grated horseradish, and, as usual, thorougly incorporate it into the mixture. The mass is filled into narrow hog casings and made into links about 4 inches long. The sausages are to be only slightly cooked.

### BOCK SAUSAGE

Take about one-third each of beef, veal and pork, chopping up fine together, adding for 100 pounds stock, 42¼ oz. salt, 3½ oz. cayenne pepper and 3½ oz. white pepper. Some use a few small dice of boiled bacon. Fill the mass into narrow sheep casings and twist off into pairs to weigh about 4 oz. Smoke the sausages in hot smoke until they appear of a light yellow color.

### BOCK SAUSAGE—ANOTHER RECIPE

Use 60 pounds beef and 20 pounds veal, freed from thick sinews, and chop up together until very fine; 20 pounds of pork trimmings are now added, and the mixture again chopped until the mass is uniform, when sufficient water to make it moderately soft is put in. Season with 42 oz. salt, 2¾ oz. saltpetre, 6 $\frac{3}{10}$ oz. white pepper, 1¾ oz. cloves and 1 oz. either of coriander seed or garlic, whichever flavor may be desired.

After the seasoning is well kneaded in, add to the mass 12 pounds finely cut fat, which is uniformly mixed with the other ingredients. Fill the mass into narrow beef casings and make short sausages, which are smoked until they are brownish red. The sausages are boiled when prepared for the table.

### FRICADELLEN

Use shoulder pork and lean pork trimmings, which should be freed from any sinews and soft fat. Chop moderately fine. Stir up one-quarter pound wheat flour with cold water and mix with this two eggs. Use this quantity of flour and eggs to every 10 pounds of meat. No water should be added to the mass itself. Season with 4¼ oz. salt, seven-eighths of an ounce of white pepper and one-tenth ounce mace. Knead the mass well and from it form cakes of 2 to 3 oz. weight. Each cake is then wrapped in a piece of hog caul, which has previously been well soaked and freed from fat. The wrapper should be of sufficient size to just contain the cake.

They are placed on a dish, the folded side down, and garnished with parsley. They are to be fried in butter when served for the table.

### FRENCH FRICADELLES

These are made with 70 parts lean pork and 30 parts firm fat, generally back fat. The mixture is chopped fine and seasoned with 3¾ oz. salt, three-quarters of an ounce of white pepper, one-tenth ounce ground cardamom seed, and 3 tablespoonfuls orange water. The mass is kneaded to a stiff paste with a little water, and then treated as in former recipe.

### BRAIN SAUSAGE

To 4 pounds finely chopped veal add 10 pounds fat belly pork and 3 or 4 pounds well cleaned brain freed from the skin. The brain is cut into small dice before adding to the meat; 3 or 4 large onions are sliced, added to the mixture, and the whole chopped fine. For each 10 pounds use as seasoning 5 oz. salt, two-thirds of an ounce pepper, one-fifth ounce allspice and one-tenth ounce cloves. Mix well and stuff into narrow hog or beef bung guts, making into small rounded sausages. Allow them to dry several days, after which put in cold smoke until they are of a light brown color.

This sausage should be made in limited quantities, as it will not keep for a great length of time. It is most largely made in cold weather.

### BRAIN SAUSAGE—ANOTHER RECIPE

To every 4 pounds fat pork chopped moderately fine is added 1 pound brain, prepared as usual for this purpose. One-half pound wheat bread is well soaked in milk, the excess squeezed out and added to the mixture. The whole is well mixed and chopped fine. For every 10 pounds of mass, spice as follows: 3¼ oz. salt, one-half ounce pepper,

70 grains nutmeg, and 30 grains cassia-buds. It is filled loosely into narrow hog or sheep casings, their whole length.

The sausage is then well washed with water and coiled up in a dish. This gives it a peculiar shape, fancied by some trade.

### KIDNEY SAUSAGE

Two well cleaned hog kidneys are finely chopped before adding the other ingredients. Two pounds of pork, of which about one-quarter is fat, is then put with the chopped kidneys and this mixture is again chopped. Season the mass with 3¼ oz. salt, one-half ounce pepper, one-tenth ounce allspice and 1 tablespoonful of red wine. Knead well, and stuff into narrow hog casings to their full length and then treat the filled casings the same as in preceding recipe.

It is necessary in making this sausage to first chop the kidneys by themselves, as they will not be of the required fineness if chopped up with the meat.

### SMOKED KIDNEY SAUSAGE

To each 10 pounds of fat pork add 30 or 40 cooked hog kidneys, which have been previously very finely chopped. The mixed meats are now chopped up together; to the above add 4 pounds lean pork. This should be chopped fine before placing with the rest of the meat. Season the mass with 3¾ oz. salt, one-half ounce white pepper and one-sixth ounce allspice, and fill loosely into beef bung guts, making rounded sausages by the usual method. Cook them in water kept at 95° F., remove and allow them to cool. Smoke for 1 or 2 days in cold smoke. These sausages are prepared for table use by cooking 1 or 2 minutes.

Sometimes kidneys have a rather strong odor which is

very objectionable. A good way to remove the peculiar warm, damp smell from such kidneys is to first cleanse them well in plenty of clean water, then place in a tub with 4 oz. of quick-lime to 1 pound of water or about one-half ounce of soda ash to 1 quart of water, and let them remain there until the odor is removed.

### ROLLEPÖHSE (GEORGE SAUSAGE)

Beef firm and rather fat, from young cattle, is used for this. The meat is trimmed free of bone and sinews and cut into half-inch squares. For each 10 pounds beef add 1½ pounds bacon, also cut into half-inch squares. Chop up fine. For 100 pounds mass, season as follows: 53 oz. salt, 5¼ oz. white pepper, 1¾ oz. allspice and seven-eighths ounce cloves. Mix up well, knead to a stiff paste and allow it to remain in this condition for 24 hours. Meanwhile make small bags from well-cleaned beef cauls about 4 inches wide by 6 inches long, leaving in them an opening for filling.

After the mass has remained the necessary time, it is again kneaded and then stuffed rather tightly into the small bags, which are sewed up and placed in a vessel with sufficient water to cover them. The water is then heated to boiling and kept simmering for 3 hours; any scum forming on the water is removed. The sausages, after the required cooking, are allowed to cool in the same water or broth, in the cooking vessel or in a wooden tub.

When cold they are tightly packed in an earthenware jar or crock and covered with a mixture made of 1 part of broth and 3 parts of vinegar. To this mixture is added a few bay leaves and a few sliced lemons. After remaining in the covered jars for 5 or 6 days, they are ready for the market.

### OLDENBURGER RULKEN

Young fat beef is cut up after the same manner as for Rollepöhse. Scald 13 pounds best rice with boiling water, taking care not to boil the rice to a paste. Allow this to cool thoroughly, and when cold add it to the beef. Season the mixture with 50 oz. salt, 3¼ oz. white pepper and 1¾ oz. allspice. Knead the seasoning well into the mass and stuff tightly into bags made from cauls, but double the size of those used for Rollepöhse. Sew up the bags and cook slowly for 3 hours; allow them to cool in the broth. Afterwards put them in earthenware jars containing a mixture of equal parts of broth and vinegar, and allow them to remain in this for 6 or 7 days.

### BERLINER BLOOD SAUSAGE

For 100 pounds use 70 pounds raw firm bacon, 16 pounds skins, 15 pounds fresh hog blood. The bacon is cut into very small dice and scalded. It is then mixed with 16 pounds finely chopped skin and the 15 pounds fresh, strained hog blood. The mixture is spiced with 1 pound salt, 14 oz. ground white pepper, 3½ oz. ground cloves, 7 oz. allspice, three-quarters ounce marjoram and 4 oz. boracic acid. The ingredients are well mixed and stuffed loosely into middle guts. The sausages are scalded for 1 hour in water at 200° F. Any air remaining in them is removed by pricking through the casings with a fine awl or similar instrument, when, on being pressed, a rattling sound is noticed, the sausage is sufficiently cooked. They are removed from the boiling vat, dried in the ordinary temperature for 24 hours and then placed in cold smoke. This sausage is said to keep indefinitely.

### BEST BLOOD SAUSAGE

For 100 pounds stock take 46 pounds fat butts, 26

pounds pork rind and 28 pounds well agitated and stirred hog blood. The pork rinds are boiled soft and chopped up fine and added with the hog blood to the chopped butts. The mass is well incorporated and kneaded and seasoned as follows: 1¼ oz. cloves, 1½ oz. marjoram, three-quarters ounce thyme, 10 oz. black pepper, 2 pounds chopped onions and 1½ pounds salt.

This mixture is well incorporated and is stuffed into beef bungs, cooked in water 200° F., and then smoked.

### COMMON BLOOD SAUSAGE

For this may be used all sorts of trimmings, skins, etc., from any kind of meat. The material is put into bags and boiled until soft. For a general recipe (which may be modified to suit price and other conditions) use 60 pounds sinews and meat trimmings, 12 pounds skins, 12 pounds bacon trimmings and 16 pounds hog or beef blood.

The skins are first finely chopped, then the trimmings and sinews added and coarsely chopped. The bacon trimmings are cut in small dice, scalded, drained and incorporated with the mass.

Season with 17½ oz. salt, 15¾ oz. black pepper, 1⅛ oz. marjoram and 3¾ oz. boracic acid.

If the sinews or trimmings should have a slight smell, a further flavoring of 1 oz. crushed juniper berries should be added to the mass and well distributed through it. To the whole mixture is now added the well-agitated and strained blood, and the mass again kneaded thoroughly.

Stuff into narrow beef casings, and cook the sausages in hot water about 200° F. Remove and put into cold water. When cold, wipe dry and smoke for about 12 hours.

### BLOODWURST

Chop 90 pounds fat pork into small cubes or dice and

add to it 10 pounds finely-chopped cheek meat. Add to the mass the necessary amount of well-agitated hog blood to make the desired consistency for stuffing. For 100 pounds of mixture add as seasoning, 30 oz. salt, 6 oz. black pepper, 1 oz. coriander seed, 4 oz. marjoram and 2 oz. allspice. Mix thoroughly and stuff mass in beef middles, adding 3 or 4 pieces of hog tongue to each sausage.

### JAUER SAUSAGE

The mass for this is made of pork. In every 100 pounds may be 20 or 25 pounds of fat or bacon. Large or thick sinews and any soft fat must be carefully removed. Chop the material fine and season with $35\frac{1}{4}$ oz. salt, $7\frac{1}{10}$ oz. white pepper, three-quarters ounce ground cloves and a small quantity of lemon peel, chopped very fine. Water is kneaded into the mass until of the desired consistency. Stuff into beef bungs in the manner indicated.

Genuine Jauer sausages are always stuffed in beef bungs. The casings are carefully scalded in water just below the boiling point and are then blown up to their full extent, tieing them while in this shape. The empty casings hung on sticks, are dried and then smoked until of a light brown color. Before using, the tied ends are cut off and the other part of the casings soaked in warm water, until soft and pliable.

In stuffing always use the whole piece, closing the end with a small wooden skewer. A string noose is made on each end, by which to hang the sausage for drying.

### JAUER SAUSAGE—ANOTHER RECIPE

In some localities sausage made by the following recipe is much favored:

To 50 pounds beef trimmings freed from sinews 25 pounds fat pork trimmings are added. First chop the beef for 45 minutes, then add the pork and continue the chopping for 15 minutes more. Then add the seasoning, 31½ oz. salt, 28¼ oz. black pepper, 2 1/10 oz. allspice and three-quarters ounce ground cinnamon. Continue chopping a quarter of an hour longer, knead the mass well, fill into narrow hog casings and twist off in pairs, 5 to 6 inches in length. Dry in a good draft and put in cold smoke for 3 or 4 days. In summer, if not wanted for immediate consumption, 2 oz. borax may be added to the mass as a preserva-

### STUFFED PARISIAN HOG'S HEAD

Select a well-shaped head, cut off about 3 to 4 pounds behind the ears; now remove the bones, care to be taken, especially above the eyes, where the skin is thinnest and lies right on the bone; do not remove the snout bones, only saw off the hindmost jawbone right behind the mouth. Remove the cheek meat on either side, until with the skin, it is about half an inch thick. Cut off about 3 inches square from lower cheek at the back to make the head more shapely.

Now sew from the snout up to the back opening where the head is to be filled, cut around over from the skin to fit the back opening. Now prepare the stuffing as follows:

Good, firm, young pork, moderately fat, is coarsely chopped with 5¼ oz. salt and allowed to stand 24 hours; use 10 pounds, chop fine, add 4 shallots, roasted in butter, rubbed up with a pinch of salt. Spice with one-half ounce finely ground white pepper, 77 grains finely ground mace, two handfuls green peeled pistaches and 1 to 1½ oz. white Perigord truffles, cut into dice.

Also mix red, salted, boiled tongues, cut into half-inch squares; mix all well and fill the head with it. Sew the cover on, smoke for 2 hours or until yellow brown; tie up tightly in muslin; tie a string around it very evenly from front to rear. Now cook in boiling water 3 to 3½ hours and then allow to cool. Dip the ears in hot water; put a few sticks in front of them to keep them upright while cooling. The head should be of a chestnut brown color. Cut out the eyes, fill them with lard, and put in juniper berries, to mark the pupils. Put a lemon and some green bay leaves into the mouth, and make a nice trimming with red and white jelly and lard.

### PARISIAN JELLY

Use well trimmed pig skins freed from all fat, scrape them clean, put into a copper vessel and add enough warm water to cover well; heat, stirring constantly until the liquid becomes cloudy or turbid. Now pour off the turbid water, wash again with a little warm water, then add hot water. For three pints of water use 1 pound of skins or 1½ pounds scalded calves' feet. In order to render the jelly stronger and more palatable, add 1 pound lean beef; then add for this quantity:

One and a quarter oz. salt, 2 slices lemon, 8 large grains of pepper, 2 cloves put into an onion, 1 carrot, one-half celery root, 1 wineglassful vinegar.

Boil in a small vessel, take it from the fire, put on hot stove or steam table and allow to simmer quietly until the skins are soft; let cool and skim off the fat. Warm the jelly up somewhat, to make it liquid. Beat up whites of 3 eggs, add to the jelly, put it upon a low fire and stir slowly. When the jelly begins to form waves, take from fire, uncover, put upon a hot plate or steam table, raising one side by placing a block underneath, and allow to simmer slowly for half an hour. Now strain through fine muslin; sometimes it is also strained through filter paper, into a porcelain or earthenware vessel. It should be filled into the mould when lukewarm, not hot; if it is desired to color the jelly use a vegetable color—cochineal, violet or orange yellow. Always allow the jelly to cool thoroughly. To remove it, dip the form into warm water for a second, up to the rim. When the jelly has become loosened, shake more or less violently a few times, put the dish on top and turn over immediately; then the mould is slowly lifted. If the jelly is wanted for immediate use, the best table gelatine should be used. Clarify and boil as with skin jelly. The copper vessel used for this should have a strong bottom. Jelly should be clear enough to allow writing to be read through it with ease.

### PARISIAN HAM SAUSAGE

For 100 pounds use one-third beef and two-thirds pork ham or shoulder moderately fat, and coarsely chop each separately, adding $3\frac{1}{3}$ pounds fine salt, $5\frac{1}{4}$ oz. cane sugar, and $2\frac{3}{8}$ oz. powdered saltpetre. Mix one-third of the spicing with the beef, two-thirds with the pork, and keep each kind of meat separate; in summer allow it to remain for 12 hours in a cool room, in winter for 2 or 3 days, at about 72° F. to give it a good red color. Then first chop the beef fine, adding the pork and also the spicing before chopping both up together. Use 5 oz. white pepper, ground; $1\frac{4}{10}$ oz. fine ginger, ground; $1\frac{4}{10}$ oz. mace, $1\frac{3}{4}$ oz. finely ground allspice, sifted; 10 pieces of leek finely ground up with salt.

Mix the spice in a suitable dish, and add to the whole mass, and now chop (continually mixing the mass) to the size of a pea, so that the whole assumes a marbled appearance. Now mix a little water to it, if required, and break open the mass several times. If the meat is not very firm and does not work well, add some more meat, about 20 or 25 pounds. Fill the mass into veal bladders or in moderately wide beef guts or middle guts. Stuff airtight and firm. When stuffed, allow to hang in the air in summer for 6 hours at about 70° F. to give it a lasting color.

Now smoke in regular smoke at 77° F. until the sausages are cherry red; boil immediately after smoking, using the water at the boiling point. The bladders take from three-quarters to 1 hour to cook, while the beef guts should boil gently for 1½ to 1¾ hours, avoiding agitation as much as possible, as much agitation will tear the sausage casings. This sausage should, therefore, never be boiled with others requiring a stronger scalding, but always by itself. When cold, this sausage usually shows wrinkles; to remove them, dip the sausage for 10 seconds in boiling water; take out and wipe dry with a cloth. Finally it is rubbed with a little cottonseed oil to make it glossy. This sausage is very popular in certain localities, and can be manufactured even in very hot weather.

### DECORATED HAM

Hams fresh from the smoke with a soft skin are best adapted for this purpose. Cook the ham, let cool, trim it nicely all around, and uncover the bone enough to fasten the cuff to it. Now cut little squares into the skin at the front part, all around at equal distance from the edge. Then fill the empty squares with white lard, smooth with the knife, so that the skin shows again. Now carve out some kind of ornament, such as a star, from red or white jelly. Hash up a little more jelly to make it look like diamonds and put along the edge of the star; make a border around same of laurel and lemon; then make some fancy painting with lard on the empty places of the skin.

Put a paper cuff around the bone, such as can be bought

in stationery stores. Take several colors—white, red, golden, green, pink, blue, etc., when several hams are to be decorated.

### BAYONNE HAM

From a freshly slaughtered lean pig the tenderloins (which lie along either side of the back bone) are taken and cut out lengthwise as whole as possible. They are then trimmed round, in the shape of a sausage. They are then rubbed with hot salt and placed in a dish containing cold brine. The latter is made by boiling 1 pound of salt in 2 quarts of water.

The meat should be entirely covered with brine and remain in it for 2 weeks.

The tenderloins are then taken out and washed, put in beef bungs and wrapped tightly with twine. They should be smoked for 2 weeks.

This ham is esteemed a great delicacy.

### BAYONNE BLADDER HAM

Cut the neck cutlets down to the sixth rib, take out the bones, remove the outer layer of fat, remove the meat from the five ribs down to the thick part, so as to leave the round, nice, lean lump of neck cutlet meat; rub with fine salt and put layer of salt between each layer of meat; pour in sufficient aromatic brine to cover the meat, leaving an inch of the liquid on top, weight down somewhat and allow to remain in the brine from 8 to 10 days, according to thickness of the meat; after that take out and, when not needed for immediate use, let the meat remain piled dry 4 or 5 days in a heap, to make it more juicy.

Press the material with the hands into a nice round shape, put into beef guts, not too wet; tie lengthwise and then wind the string around them, beginning from the thicker end; the rolls to be about one-third of an inch apart, having the casing fit tightly. Make a noose on one end, put a stick through the casing to avoid dropping out, and tie the stick also. Now put all the hams into boiling water for 8 to 10 seconds, taking care to pierce the casings previously for any air bubbles.

Hang up in a dry place until the hams appear like a dry bladder. In winter use a room at about 68° to 72° F.; then put in smoke rather high. Smoke like cervelat sausage, adding juniper berries. When smoked the hams are stored in a cool, airy place. When sliced they look marbled, cherry-red, have a nice taste, and are very tender.

### NORTH OF ENGLAND WHITE PUDDING

To every 6 pounds of groats use 6 pounds of leaf lard, chopped to about the size of a nut. The groats should be boiled for about 30 minutes; add the seasoning to the puddings while hot, and 4 quarts of fresh milk. Mix the whole thoroughly and knead well together. Fill into skins, and boil for about 20 minutes in clear water.

A good seasoning for white puddings is made by mixing from 6 to 8 oz. of fine salt with every pound of the finest ground white pepper. No herbs must be used. Use of the seasoning, from 6 to 8 oz. to every 12 pounds of groats.

### FINEST MORTADELLI—(DUTCH STYLE)

Can be made in summer in the hottest weather. For 100 pounds use $56\frac{3}{4}$ pounds pork, lean, from hams of light, firm hogs; $26\frac{1}{2}$ pounds lean, well trimmed young beef from neck or shoulder; $16\frac{1}{2}$ pounds fresh, white fat cut into dice about one-eighth of an inch.

The above meat is previously chopped up, together with 53 oz. fine salt, $4\frac{3}{4}$ oz. cane sugar and $2\frac{1}{10}$ oz. powdered potassium saltpetre. Mix the seasoning well and add thereof two-thirds to the pork and one-third to the beef.

Chop the beef fine, the pork more coarsely; then press together and leave at rest in an earthenware vessel for 2 days. Then chop both kinds of meat together very fine. Now spice as follows: 4¾ oz. fine white pepper, 1$\frac{1}{10}$ oz. fine white ginger, 1 $\frac{1}{10}$ oz. mace, 10 pieces of shallots rubbed up fine with salt. The mixed spice is added to the mass; also if desired 6 to 10 pounds beef or veal previously pounded into a kind of jelly with wooden mallets, as explained under substitute for starch. Knead all up together, add a little water to make the mass easier to handle. When worked for a quarter of an hour, add the lard dice; knead 15 minutes more and break the mass open several times to make it uniform, without mashing the fat, until the mass appears firm.

Put into sausage machine, press down firmly to avoid air bubbles. Fill into beef bung guts, well dried, 12 to 16 inches long or use large, narrow calf bladders, or long, narrow cow bladders, and stuff tightly.

Now allow to dry, in winter, 48 hours in a warm room at 77° F. Smoke evenly, in warm smoke, using beech or oak shavings mixed with a few juniper leaves. Let the sausages stand until they are a cherry red, then put into tank and scald; those in butt ends to be treated 1¾ hours, those very thick, for 2 hours. Scald without having the water boil. When done, on taking the mortadelli out of the tub, the water should run off immediately, leaving the skin perfectly dry. Put into coarse muslin until perfectly cool, when they will be bright red and will retain this color.

### ITALIAN MORTADELLI

Six pounds raw, lean pork, 4 pounds veal, both free from sinews, 5 pounds pickled, then boiled, pork from back, all chopped up fine. Now add 1¼ pounds chopped sardines, freed from bones, 5¼ oz. pistaches, freed from shells, 3 oz. white pepper, 4 to 5½ oz. salt, 5¼ oz. capers, 2 tablespoonfuls best Jamaica rum, 2½ pounds raw back fat, cut into small dice, and 6 to 8 pickled, boiled pig tongues, cut into strips, from which the white skin has been previously removed.

Now treat as in the former recipe and wind string all around as for roulade.

### SWISS LANDJAEGER

Eighteen pounds of lean pork and 12 pounds of fat belly are chopped up with salt and 1 oz. saltpetre, and sufficient water added to make a stiff mass. Add 1¾ oz. white pepper, three-quarters ounce caraway seed and one-third ounce mace. Also a little garlic. Stuff loosely into narrow beef casings and twist off in pairs. Now put all the sausage on a table side by side, keeping the loose ends of the casings folded under the sausage to prevent the mass escaping when pressed. Now put a board on top, weight it down and press for 1 or 2 days until the sausage is flat and square. Smoke in cold smoke until brown and hard.

### GOOSE LIVER GALANTINE

For batches of 10 pounds use 10 pounds young, fat pork from fore or hind leg without too much fat, and half of the belly, and chop fine. Then roast 4 shallots in fresh butter to a light yellow, rub fine with a pinch of salt and add to the mass. Then take 5½ oz. fine salt, one-half ounce finely ground white pepper, 62 grains white ginger, 62 grains mace, 31 grains fine thyme and 46 grains dried mushrooms. Mix with the mass and season to taste.

For wrapping the mass use a belly from which the ribs have been cut; take two slices about one-fifth of an inch thick; use a large, thick, sharp knife, dipping it into hot water before slicing. Place the slice upon the table, put about three-quarters of an inch of the mass upon it, and leave a piece of about 4 inches uncovered right and left. Now put upon the first layer of the mass a layer of well-salted boiled tongue. Cut into dice about one-half walnut size in the middle. On each side of the tongue put white goose livers, each liver being cut into four pieces; truffles are also added, about one-half inch in thickness. Boiled green pistaches should now be placed with the rest of the material, the different articles side by side. Now cover with a second layer of the mass, and upon that put again tongues, large pieces of goose liver with truffles and pistaches among them. Cover once more with mass. Now fold the two overlapping pieces of belly together over the whole. Put all into a piece of muslin, tie up well and treat like a roulade. Simmer at 205° F. in batches of 3 to 3½ pounds for 2 to 2½ hours, according to thickness.

Allow to cool for 8 to 10 hours, making sure that it is thoroughly chilled. Loosen the strings, take off the cloth very carefully and the beautiful galantine will be seen white in a skin of meat without any casing. It will remain juicy and appetizing almost indefinitely.

### CALF SWEETBREAD GALANTINE

This galantine is especially liked for its fine flavor and beautiful appearance. For 10 pounds use 10 pounds of young, firm pork from hind or fore leg, and half of the belly, moderately fat, and chop very fine. Now roast 4 shallots in fresh butter to a light yellow, rub them fine with a pinch of salt, and add to the mass. Now take 5¼ oz. fine salt, one-half ounce best white ground pepper, 77 grains finest white ginger and 77 grains mace. Mix with the mass. Now prepare the envelope from the bellies, as described under the recipe for goose liver galantine. Two slices of the jelly will generally suffice. Put the slice on the table. Put on the meat about three-quarters of a pound of filling, and leave again right and left about 4 inches uncovered to be used for a cover. Now put on the first layer—one of nicely salted boiled tongue right in the middle; to the right and left of it put well scalded calf sweetbreads in their whole thickness; next put truffle and scalded pistaches. Upon this comes another layer of the mass, on which is put again tongue, sweetbreads, intermixed with truffles and pistaches, covered by another layer of the mass. Then fold up the two slices left uncovered right and left into a piece of muslin, tie up in batches of 3 to 3½ pounds and scald at 200° F. for 2 to 2½ hours, according to thickness. When boiled allow to cool slowly 8 to 10 hours. Then remove first the string and loosen the cloth from the sides carefully.

### LACHS SCHLINKEN

Take a hog back or rather two caslet pieces from full, heavy hogs, trim off all the lean meat, including the tenderloins, from the caselet to the ham, take out all the bones, and put into aromatic pickle for 6 days. Then take them out of the pickle, wash well with fresh water, allow to drain, and wind one part upon the other, placing the sides where bones were on the inside; the fat side to be the outer side. Now put into fresh or well soaked beef-guts, press the contents together, tie up well and wind thin string around, the rolls to be about one-third of an inch apart. A very long string is now wound around a stick, a loop made in it and the thickest end of the roulade placed into it. Now wind the string, turning the roulade with the left hand and pressing it against the table, while the right hand tightens the string. Great care has to be taken to tie it evenly, as otherwise the sausage will become curved. The whole length of the roulade is about 16 to 18 inches. It also has to be well punctured to remove the air. Now let dry for several days in the open air, then smoke lightly, with juniper berries, until of light yellow color.

### BOLOGNA SAUSAGE

The meat used in this is generally pickled. Use 62° pickle, adding 1 pound saltpetre to each tierce and pickle for about 14 hours.

Take out and drain meat in any practicable manner (generally over night), previous to chopping.

Take one-half hearts and one-half cheek meat, pork and beef, adding as much of other meats, rough trimmings, etc., as is consistent with the sale price of the bologna.

To each 100 pounds mixture add, when about half chopped, 10 oz. black pepper, 6 oz. ground cloves, 2 oz. coriander seed and 4 oz. saltpetre. Mix well and chop very fine.

Use beef middle guts, 12 to 14 inches long, which, when stuffed, form the necessary rings. Smoke nicely, after which cook in hot water, about 160° to 170° F. for about 30 minutes or until fairly hard.

Use 1 pint of color to each 40 gallons of water. This gives a good color to the casings.

Hang the sausages in a cool, dry place, and when cold wipe well with a damp cloth, or a cloth saturated with cottonseed oil.

### BOLOGNA SAUSAGE—ANOTHER RECIPE

For this may be used all fresh stock. Take fresh pork and beef hearts, cheek meat and any kind of fresh trimmings not wanted for other uses. The proportion of this stock may be varied according to circumstances. For 100 pounds mass, use 2 pounds of potato flour and season with 30 oz. salt, 2 oz. saltpetre, 10 oz. black pepper, 6 oz. allspice, 2 oz. ground ginger and 2 oz. coriander seed. Chop the whole together fine and mix well. May be stuffed as in previous recipe to form rings or put into large beef casings. Smoked and cooked as usual. When large casings are used, a longer time will be required for cooking, but the temperature of the water should not be higher than 170° F.

### GERMAN BOLOGNA SAUSAGE

Take 16 pounds of beef, 8 pounds of veal or pork, 8 pounds of back fat, 4 pounds of flour, 4 pounds of sausage meal, 11 oz. of salt, 2 oz. of saltpetre, 4 oz. of white pepper and 1 oz. of coriander seed, ground, with salt. After cutting all the meats into about two-inch squares, put into the chopping machine, and chop very fine. Scald the flour previous to use, then add it slowly, along with the sausage meal. The other ingredients to be incorporated in the same manner, except the back fat, which should be previously prepared by cutting into half inch squares with the fat cutter. Use beef casings and simmer (not boil) for 3 hours in water-jacketed kettle. Before removing them add 4 oz. of brown German dye. The dye is fixed on the casings by transferring the sausage to a vat of cold water into which 2 pounds of alum have been dissolved. This quantity of alum is sufficient for 100 pounds of water.

### POLISH SAUSAGE

For 100 pounds stock use 53 pounds beef chuck meat, 10 pounds fresh pork trimmings, 24 pounds salt pork, 10 pounds fresh pork cheeks and 3 pounds fat pork butts. Chop all together moderately fine (or it may be coarsely chopped for some trade) and season with 6 oz. white pepper, 1 oz. saltpetre and 8 oz. borax. Thoroughly mix, as usual, and stuff in hog casings. Make into double links about 8 or 10 inches long, and smoke from 2 to 2½ hours over a hot fire.

If desired a slight garlic flavor may be given these.

### WESTPHALIEN SAUSAGE

Take 16 pounds of beef, 8 pounds of veal or pork, 8 pork to make 100 pounds stock. Cut the material into very small dice or cubes and season with 42 oz. salt and 14 oz. ground pepper. Mix thoroughly and stuff into narrow hog casings. The ends should be tied together.

Smoke for 7 or 8 days over a low fire. They are then hung up in an airy place, where they will keep in good condition for a long time. The sausages are prepared for the table by boiling or frying.

### SUMMER SAUSAGE

Use 37½ lbs. lean beef, 37½ lbs. lean pork and 25 lbs. back fat or fat pork. Chop the whole fine and add as seasoning, while chopping, 32 oz. salt, 2 oz. powdered saltpetre, 10 oz. ground white pepper, 3 oz. whole coriander seed and 2 oz. whole mustard seed.

Stuff the mass into hog bungs which have been well soaked overnight and washed thoroughly, leaving on the "crown." With the meats for this sausage put no water, but allow them to drain well before using. This is aided by spreading the meats and sprinkling them with salt.

Stuff slowly into the hog bungs, taking care to leave no vacant spaces in the casing. A cold, slow smoking is essential to producing a fine appearing sausage. Cool, dry storage is also necessary for this sausage.

The above recipe will answer for cervelat, and also, when the stock is chopped coarse, for salami.

The addition of a small quantity of coloring matter, "sausage color," will give a bright color to the meats, which they will retain while being cured.

Sometimes, after the meats are chopped sufficiently, a few ounces of whole peppers are added to the mass and the whole chopped again for a short time. This latter method is practiced in some localities where the summer sausage made in this manner is preferred to that without the chopped peppers being added.

### CAMBRIDGE SAUSAGE

Take 75 lbs. pork trimmings, and 75 lbs. veal and add to these while chopping 4 loaves of bread which have been previously prepared as directed, for use as filler. Season the mass as follows: One-quarter pound mace, one-quarter pound cloves, one-quarter pound cinnamon, one-quarter pound nutmeg, one-half pound white pepper, one-quarter pound marjoram, and salt to taste, which may be, for the above quantity, about 4 pounds.

Stuff the mass, when thoroughly mixed, into sheep casings.

### BULK SAUSAGE

This may be prepared in a few minutes, with a small hand chopper. For 30 lbs. use two-thirds lean and one-third fat pork, and add as seasoning, one-half pound salt, 2½ oz. pepper and 1 oz. marjoram, rubbed fine. If desired, in addition to the above seasoning, 2 oz. rubbed sage may also be added.

## SEASONINGS

It is often very desirable and convenient to have seasonings for the different kinds of sausages already prepared and mixed.

To save time and many weighings of small quantities of ingredients, the following mixtures may be prepared and the requisite weight of them added, to obtain the necessary flavor.

### FOR SUMMER SAUSAGE

34 parts salt,
11 " pepper,
3 " whole coriander seed.

Use 48 oz. per 100 pounds meat.

### FOR LIVER SAUSAGE

32 parts fine salt,
8 " white pepper,
4 " ground cloves,
1 " marjoram.

Use 45 oz. mixture per 100 pounds meat.

### FOR WIENERWURST

33 parts salt,
9 " ground white pepper.

Use 42 oz. mixture for 100 pounds meat.

### FOR BLOODWURST (BLOOD SAUSAGE)

30 parts salt,
6 " black pepper,
1 " coriander seed,
4 " marjoram,
2 " allspice.

Use 43 oz. mixture per 100 pounds stock.

### FOR HEAD CHEESE

32 parts fine salt,
8 " white pepper,
3 " ground cloves,
1 " cayenne pepper,

Use 44 oz. to each 100 pounds meat.

### FOR TONGUE SAUSAGE

33 parts salt,
7 " pepper,
3 " ground cloves and allspice,
1½ " ground ginger,
3 " ground marjoram.

Use 47½ oz. per 100 pounds meat.

### FOR BOLOGNA SAUSAGE

10 parts black pepper,
6 " ground cloves,
2 " coriander seed,
30 " fine salt,
2 " saltpetre,

Use 50 oz. per 100 pounds stock.

When salt meats are used in the stock, due allowance should be made for the salt, as noted elsewhere.

### FOR FRANKFORT SAUSAGE

25 parts salt,
12 " ground white pepper,

Use 37 oz. per 100 pounds meat.

### FOR SALAMI

44 parts salt,
11 " ground white pepper,
3 " saltpetre,
— garlic flavor.

Use 58 oz. per 100 pounds meat.

### FOR PORK SAUSAGE

6 parts white pepper,
1½ " cayenne pepper,
1½ " ground nutmeg and mace,
22 " fine salt.

To which may be added a small quantity of sage if so desired.

Use 32 oz. to each 100 pounds stock.

### FOR HAM, CHICKEN, AND TONGUE SAUSAGE

32 parts fine salt,
8 " white pepper,
1 " mace,
2 " cloves and allspice.

Use 43 oz. per 100 pounds meat.

The above seasonings will not suit all tastes or trade. Each maker can vary the proportions of the mixtures to suit any special trade or some localities.

In boiling all sausages, the fat or grease floating on the surface of the water should always be removed before taking the sausages from the cooking vessel. Otherwise this fat will adhere to the sausage casings and is liable to be lost.

Printed in Great Britain
by Amazon